The Super Fun Knock Knock Joke Book

Ivy Finnegan

ARCTURUS

ARCTURUS
This edition published in 2022 by Arcturus Publishing Limited
26/27 Bickels Yard, 151–153 Bermondsey Street,
London SE1 3HA

Author: Ivy Finnegan
Illustrator: Ana Bermejo
Editor: Donna Gregory
Designer: Marie Everitt
Editorial Manager: Joe Harris

Published and Distributed in India by Scholastic India Pvt. Ltd.
This Reprint Edition: February, 2025

ISBN: 978-93-5954-124-2

Printed in India at Shivam Offset Press, New Delhi

Contents

CHAPTER 1

Silly Jokes

Knock, knock ...

Who's there?

Cereal ...

Cereal who?

Cereal pleasure to meet you!

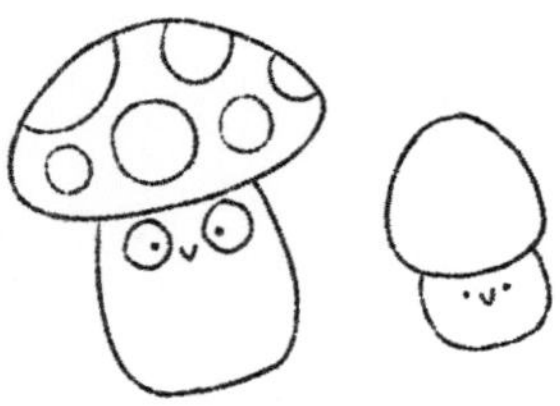

Knock, knock ...

Who's there?

Twitter.

Twitter who?

Have you got an owl in there?

KNOCK, KNOCK ...

Who's there?

LINDA ...

Linda who?

LINDA HAND TO GET THIS HEAVY SUITCASE UP THE STEPS!

knock, knock ...

Who's there?

Cheese.

Cheese who?

Cheese a cute dog!

Knock, knock ...

Who's there?

Broccoli.

Broccoli who?

Broccoli doesn't have a last name, silly.

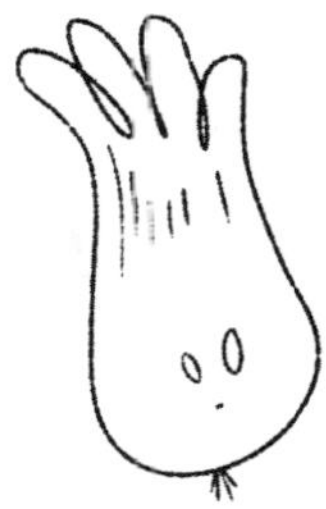

KNOCK, KNOCK ...

Who's there?

COLIN ...

Colin who?

COLIN ROUND TO SEE YOU!

Knock, knock ...

Who's there?

Denver ...

Denver who?

Denver the good old days!

KNOCK, KNOCK ...

Who's there?

KENT.

Kent who?

KENT YOU TELL BY MY VOICE?

Knock, knock ...

Who's there?

Carla ...

Carla who?

Carla me please. We need to talk.

Knock, knock ...

Who's there?

Peg ...

Peg who?

Peg your pardon, I've got the wrong door!

Knock, knock ...

Who's there?

Lauren.

Lauren who?

Lauren order!

KNOCK, KNOCK ...

Who's there?

APPLE.

Apple who?

APPLE YOUR HAIR IF YOU DON'T LET ME IN!

Knock, knock ...

Who's there?

Howie ...

Howie who?

I'm fine thanks. How are you?

Knock, knock ...

Who's there?

Doctor

Doctor who?

No, it's Doctor Strange, not Doctor Who!

Knock, knock ...

Who's there?

Arnold ...

Arnold who?

Arnold friend you haven't seen for years!

Knock, knock ...

Who's there?

Patrick.

Patrick who?

Patricked me into knocking on your door!

KNOCK, KNOCK ...

Who's there?

ELVIS.

Elvis who?

ELVIS IS A COMPLETE WASTE OF TIME, I'M OFF!

Knock, knock ...

Who's there?

Amish.

Amish who?

Amish you too!

KNOCK, KNOCK ...

Who's there?

ANDREW ...

Andrew who?

ANDREW A PICTURE FOR YOU!

Knock, knock ...

Who's there?

Lisa ...

Lisa who?

Lisa you can do is let me in!

Knock, knock ...

Who's there?

Dimension ...

Dimension who?

Dimension it!

KNOCK, KNOCK ...

Who's there?

ALVIN ...

Alvin who?

**ALVIN YOUR HEART—
JUST YOU VAIT AND SEE!**

Knock, knock ...

Who's there?

Olive ...

Olive who?

Olive you, too!

Knock, knock ...

Who's there?

India ...

India who?

**India is some of
my stuff, and I've
come to collect it!**

Knock, knock ...

Who's there?

Iona.

Iona who?

Iona have eyes for you!

Knock, knock ...

Who's there?

Daisy.

Daisy who?

Daisy plays, nights he sleeps!

Knock, knock ...

Who's there?

Sam.

Sam who?

Sam-enchanted evening!

KNOCK, KNOCK ...

Who's there?

DOT ...

Dot who?

DOTS FOR ME TO KNOW, AND YOU TO FIND OUT!

Knock, knock ...

Who's there?

Julia.

Julia who?

Julia want some milk and cookies?

Knock, knock ...

Who's there?

Avon ...

Avon who?

Avon to drink your blood!

Knock, knock ...

Who's there?

Lefty.

Lefty who?

Lefty home on your own again!

Knock, knock ...

Who's there?

Don.

Don who?

Don Patrol!

Knock, knock ...

Who's there?

Ben Hur.

Ben Hur who?

Ben Hur an hour— let me in!

Knock, knock ...

Who's there?

May ...

May who?

May the force be with you!

Knock, knock ...

Who's there?

House ...

House who?

House you doing!

Knock, knock ...

Who's there?

Dime ...

Dime who?

Dime to tell another knock, knock joke!

Knock, knock ...

Who's there?

Toby ...

Toby who?

Toby or not to be!

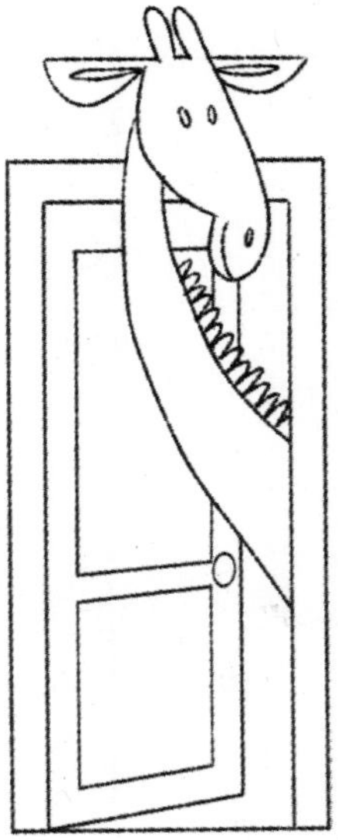

Knock, knock ...

Who's there?

Goliath ...

Goliath who?

Goliath down, you look-eth tired!

Knock, knock ...

Who's there?

Atilla ...

Atilla who?

Atilla you open this door I'm a gonna stand here!

KNOCK, KNOCK ...

Who's there?

MAXWELL ...

Maxwell who?

**MAXWELL CALL LATER—
HE ASKED ME TO LET
YOU KNOW!**

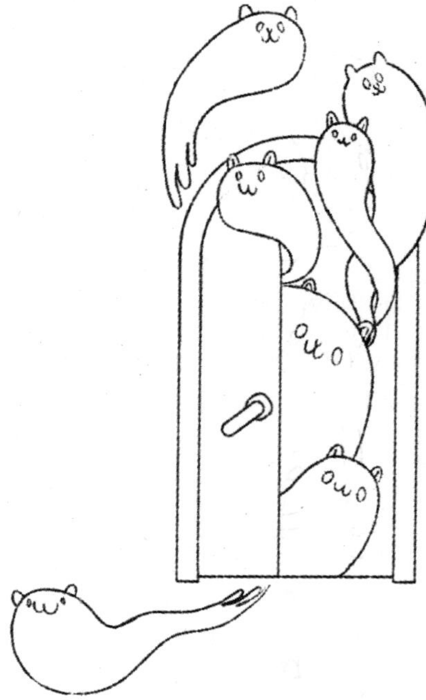

Knock, knock ...

Who's there?

Dawn ...

Dawn who?

**Dawn leave
me out here
in the cold!**

Knock, knock!

Who's there?

Al ...

Al who?

Al huff and I'll puff
and blow your
house down!

KNOCK, KNOCK ...

Who's there?

LARVA ...

Larva who?

LARVA CUP OF COFFEE, THANK YOU!

Knock, knock ...

Who's there?

Cologne ...

Cologne who?

Cologne me names won't help!

Knock, knock ...

Who's there?

Paul.

Paul who?

Paul up a chair and I'll tell you!

KNOCK, KNOCK ...

Who's there?

CHILE ...

Chile who?

CHILE OUT TONIGHT, ISN'T IT?

Knock, knock ...

Who's there?

Hutch ...

Hutch who?

Bless you!

Knock, knock ...

Who's there?

Phil.

Phil who?

Phil this bag with money, I'm a robber!

Knock, knock ...

Who's there?

Butter ...

Butter who?

Butter not leave me here much longer!

KNOCK, KNOCK ...

Who's there?

MINERVA ...

Minerva who?

MINERVA-S WRECK FROM ALL THESE QUESTIONS!

Knock, knock ...

Who's there?

Closure ...

Closure who?

Closure mouth when you're eating!

KNOCK, KNOCK ...

Who's there?

CHESTER ...

Chester who?

CHESTER THE NICK OF TIME!

Knock, knock ...

Who's there?

Luke ...

Luke who?

Luke through the keyhole and you'll see!

Knock, knock ...

Who's there?

Heaven ...

Heaven who?

Heaven seen you in ages!

Knock, knock ...

Who's there?

Gable.

Gable who?

Gable to leap buildings in a single bound!

Knock, knock ...

Who's there?

You.

You who?

You-who to you, too!

Knock, knock ...

Who's there?

CD.

CD who?

CDs fingers? They're freezing—let me in!

Knock, knock ...

Who's there?

Iowa ...

Iowa who?

Iowa you some money!

KNOCK, KNOCK ...

Who's there?

SATURN ...

Saturn who?

SATURN MY SPACESHIP, WAITING TO TAKE OFF!

Knock, knock ...

Who's there?

Disguise ...

Disguise who?

Disguise the limit!

Knock, knock ...

Who's there?

Little old lady.

Little old lady who?

I didn't know you could yodel!

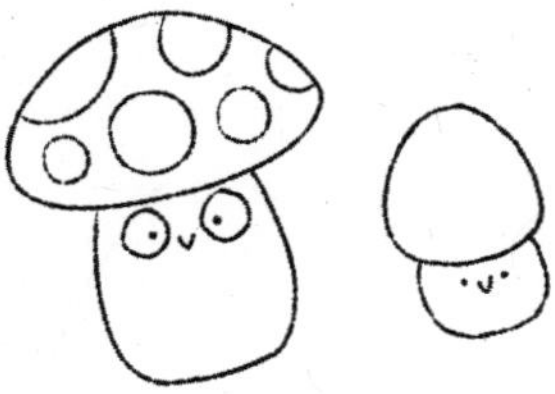

Knock, knock ...

Who's there?

Curry.

Curry who?

Curry me back home will you?

Knock, knock ...

Who's there?

Aunt Lou.

Aunt Lou who?

Aunt Lou do you think you are?

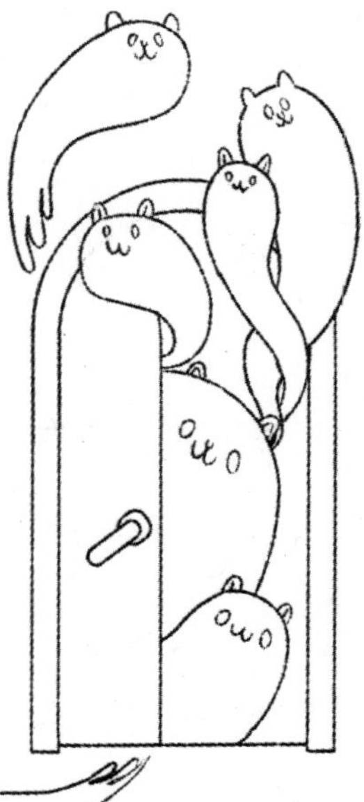

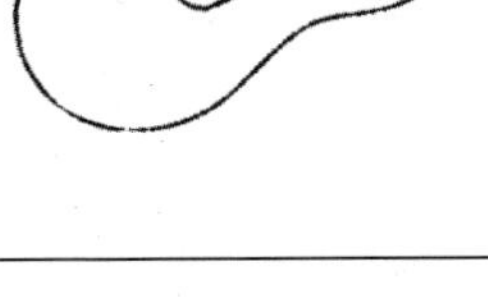

Knock, knock ...

Who's there?

Falafel ...

Falafel who?

Falafel off my bike and hurt my knee!

Knock, knock ...

Who's there?

Hanover ...

Hanover who?

Hanover your money!

Knock, knock ...

Who's there?

Ivor ...

Ivor who?

Ivor good mind not to tell you now!

KNOCK, KNOCK ...

Who's there?

JUNE ...

June who?

JUNE KNOW WHAT TIME DINNER IS?

Knock, knock ...

Who's there?

Alf ...

Alf who?

Alf feed your cat while you're away!

Knock, knock ...

Who's there?

Joan ...

Joan who?

Joan call us— we'll call you!

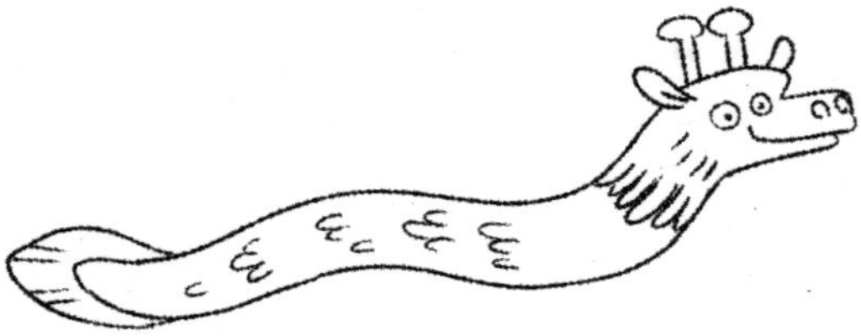

Knock, knock ...

Who's there?

Juanita ...

Juanita who?

Juanita nother burger?

Knock, knock ...

Who's there?

Ivory ...

Ivory who?

Ivory strong, just like Tarzan!

Knock, knock ...

Who's there?

Fonda ...

Fonda who?

Fonda you!

Knock, knock ...

Who's there?

Ali ...

Ali who?

Alligator. Or maybe crocodile. I can't really tell the difference!

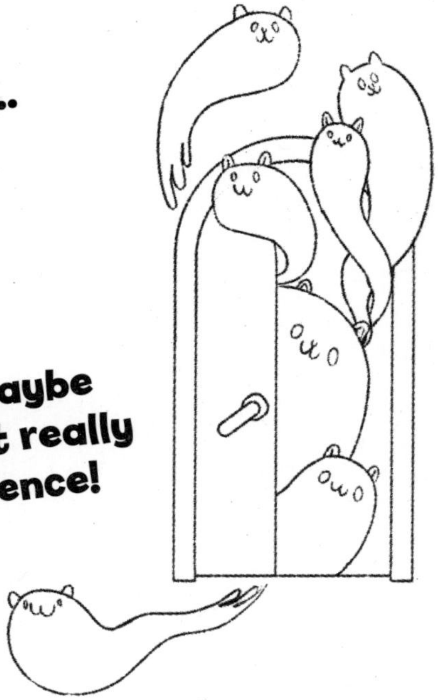

Knock, knock ...

Who's there?

Julie ...

Julie who?

Julie-ve your door unlocked?

KNOCK, KNOCK ...

Who's there?

HARMON ...

Harmon who?

HARMON ON YOUR SIDE!

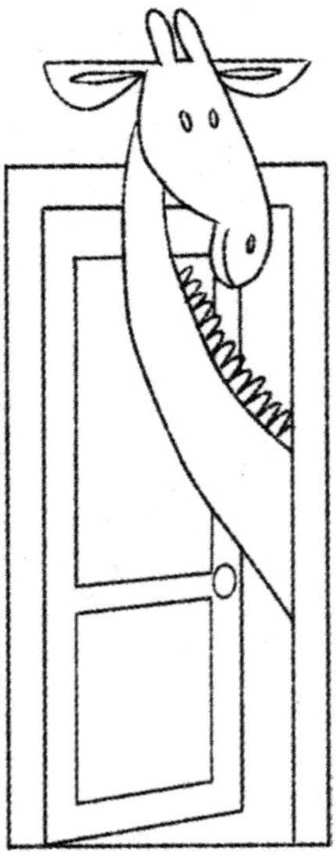

Knock, knock ...

Who's there?

Quacker ...

Quacker who?

Quacker another bad joke and I'm leaving!

Knock, knock ...

Who's there?

Gopher.

Gopher who?

Gopher help, I'm stuck in the mud!

Knock, knock ...

Who's there?

Justice ...

Justice who?

Justice as I thought, there's no-one home!

Knock, knock ...

Who's there?

Plato ...

Plato who?

Plato chicken salad, please!

Knock, knock ...

Who's there?

Eileen ...

Eileen who?

Eileen down to tie my shoe and fell over!

KNOCK, KNOCK ...

Who's there?

HAROLD ...

Harold who?

HAROLD ARE YOU?

Knock, knock ...

Who's there?

Ken ...

Ken who?

Ken I come in, or do I have to climb through a window?

Knock, knock ...

Who's there?

Eva ...

Eva who?

Eva you're deaf or your doorbell isn't working!

KNOCK, KNOCK ...

Who's there?

BETTY.

Betty who?

BETTY EARNS A LOT OF MONEY!

Knock, knock ...

Who's there?

Jaws ...

Jaws who?

Jaws truly!

KNOCK, KNOCK ...

Who's there?

IRMA ...

Irma who?

IRMA BIG GIRL NOW!

Knock, knock ...

Who's there?

Doris ...

Doris who?

Doris slammed on my finger. Ouch!

Knock, knock ...

Who's there?

Oliver ...

Oliver who?

Oliver cross the road from you!

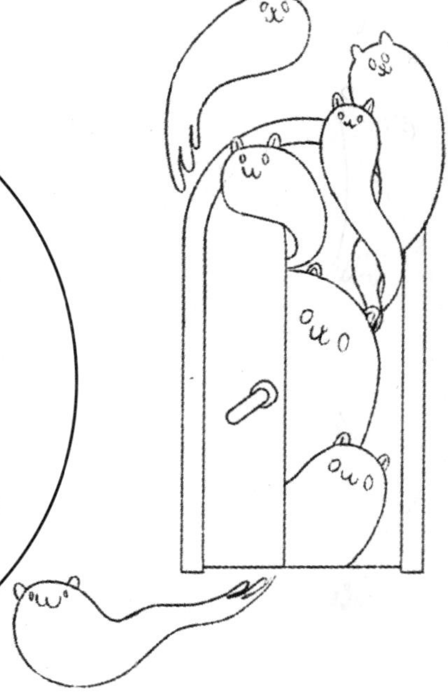

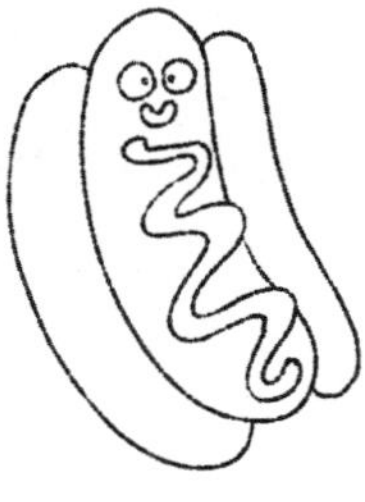

Knock, knock ...

Who's there?

Evan ...

Evan who?

Evan you should know who it is!

Knock, knock.

Who's there?

Stopwatch.

Stopwatch who?

Stopwatch you're doing and let me in!

KNOCK, KNOCK ...

Who's there?

CARMEN.

Carmen who?

CARMEN LIKE BEST IS A FERRARI!

Knock Knock ...

Who's there?

Butch, Jimmy, and Joe ...

Butch, Jimmy, and Joe who?

Butch your arms around me, Jimmy a kiss, and let's Joe!

Knock, knock ...

Who's there?

Delhi.

Delhi who?

Delhicatessen!

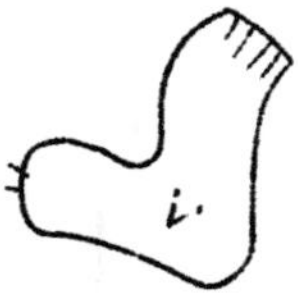

KNOCK, KNOCK ...

Who's there?

CAESAR.

Caesar who?

CAESAR JOLLY GOOD FELLOW!

Knock, knock ...

Who's there?

Blue.

Blue who?

Blue away with the wind!

Knock, knock ...

Who's there?

Boo.

Boo who?

Bootiful front door you have.

KNOCK, KNOCK

Who's there?

LION.

Lion who?

LION DOWN ON THE JOB AGAIN!

Knock, knock ...

Who's there?

Jools ...

Jools who?

Jools like these should be worth a lot of money!

Knock, knock ...

Who's there?

Dishes.

Dishes who?

Dishes the police! Open up!

KNOCK, KNOCK ...

Who's there?

PARSON.

Parson who?

PARSON THROUGH AND I THOUGHT I'D SAY HELLO!

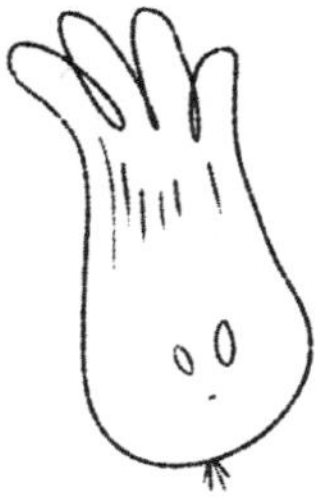

Knock, knock ...

Who's there?

Alec ...

Alec who?

Alec my lollipop, you lick yours!

Knock, knock ...

Who's there?

Isaac ...

Isaac who?

Isaac'ly who do you think this is?

Knock, knock ...

Who's there?

Zizi ...

Zizi who?

Zizi when you know how!

Knock, knock ...

Who's there?

Grant ...

Grant who?

Grant you a wish—what is it?

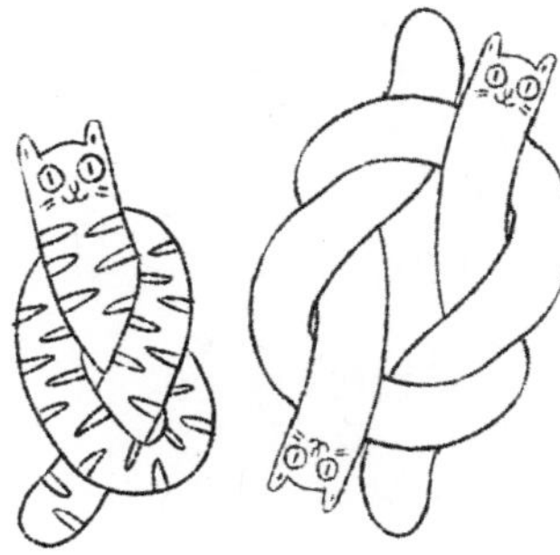

Knock, knock ...

Who's there?

Anita ...

Anita who?

Anita nother hot dog—
I'm starving!

Knock, knock ...

Who's there?

Len ...

Len who?

Len us some money, will you?

Knock, knock ...

Who's there?

Harry ...

Harry who?

Harry up! There's a monster behind us!

Knock, knock ...

Who's there?

Livia ...

Livia who?

Livia me alone!

Knock, knock ...

Who's there?

Goodunov ...

Goodunov who?

Goodunov to eat!

Knock, knock ...

Who's there?

Annie ...

Annie who?

Annie chance of getting something to drink?

Knock, knock ...

Who's there?

Aladdin ...

Aladdin who?

Aladdin the street wants a word with you!

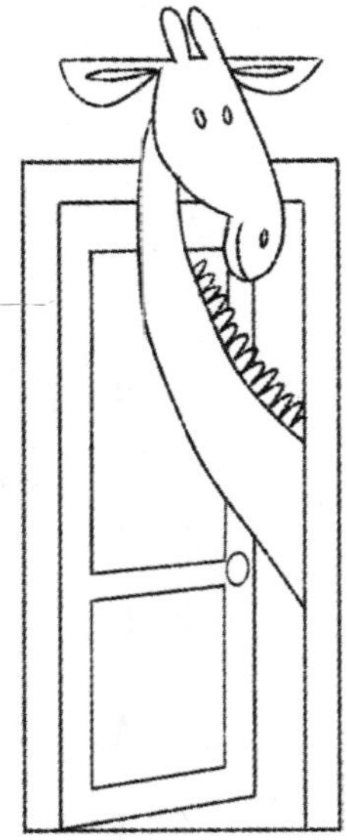

Knock, knock ...

Who's there?

Allied.

Allied who?

Allied, so sue me!

Knock, knock ...

Who's there?

Conga ...

Conga who?

Conga go on
meeting like this!

Knock, knock ...

Who's there?

Thumping.

Thumping who?

**Thumping green and slimy is
crawling up your back!**

Knock, knock ...

Who's there?

Goodunov ...

Goodunov who?

Goodunov to eat!

Knock, knock ...

Who's there?

Annie ...

Annie who?

Annie chance of getting something to drink?

Knock, knock ...

Who's there?

Aladdin ...

Aladdin who?

Aladdin the street wants a word with you!

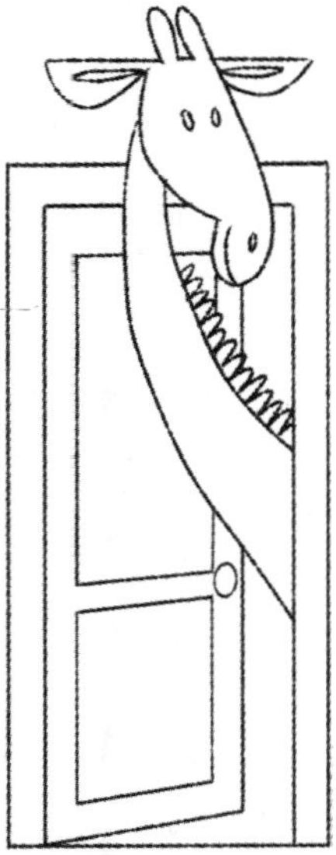

Knock, knock ...

Who's there?

ALLIED.

Allied who?

ALLIED, so sue me!

Knock, knock ...

Who's there?

Conga ...

Conga who?

Conga go on meeting like this!

Knock, knock ...

Who's there?

Thumping.

Thumping who?

Thumping green and slimy is crawling up your back!

Knock, knock ...

Who's there?

Europe ...

Europe who?

Europe-ning the door too slow, come on!

KNOCK, KNOCK ...

Who's there?

ARTHUR ...

Arthur who?

ARTHUR ANY COOKIES LEFT?

Knock, knock ...

Who's there?

Heart ...

Heart who?

Heart to hear you—speak up!

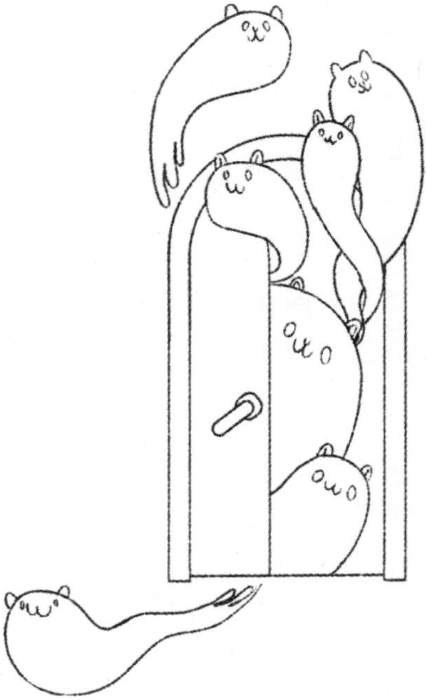

Knock, knock ...

Who's there?

Germany ...

Germany who?

Germany people knock on your door?

Knock, knock ...

Who's there?

Norway ...

Norway who?

Norway will I leave until you open this door!

Knock, knock ...

Who's there?

Major ...

Major who?

Major answer, didn't I!

Knock, knock ...

Who's there?

A woman.

A woman who?

A woman with a wooden leg.

Tell her to hop it!

Knock, knock ...

Who's there?

Maura ...

Maura who?

The Maura the merrier!

Knock, knock ...

Who's there?

Leena.

Leena who?

Leena little closer and I'll whisper in your ear!

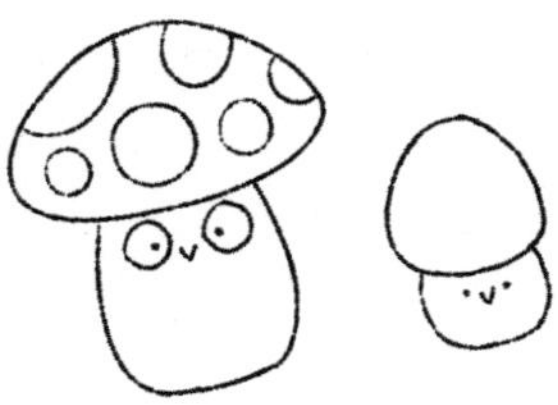

CHAPTER 2

Even Sillier Jokes

Knock, knock ...

Who's there?

Carrie ...

Carrie who?

Carrie one of these boxes for me, will you?

Knock, knock ...

Who's there?

Ice cream soda ...

Ice cream soda who?

Ice cream soda people can hear me!

Knock, knock ...

Who's there?

Amanda.

Amanda who?

Amanda fix the boiler!

Knock, knock ...

Who's there?

Sarah.

Sarah who?

Sarah bell on this door? I've been knocking for ages!

KNOCK, KNOCK ...

Who's there?

AWARE ...

Aware who?

AWARE, AWARE HAS MY LITTLE DOG GONE?

Knock, knock ...

Who's there?

Reed.

Reed who?

Reed-turn to sender, address unknown!

Knock, knock ...

Who's there?

Bill.

Bill who?

Bill-ding's on fire!

Knock, knock ...

Who's there?

Argue ...

Argue who?

Argue going to let me in or not?

Knock, knock ...

Who's there?

Tank ...

Tank who?

You're welcome!

KNOCK, KNOCK ...

Who's there?

IONA ...

Iona who?

IONA PONY. DO YOU HAVE ANY PETS?

Knock, knock ...

Who's there?

Cathy ...

Cathy who?

Cathy the doorbell, it's too dark out here!

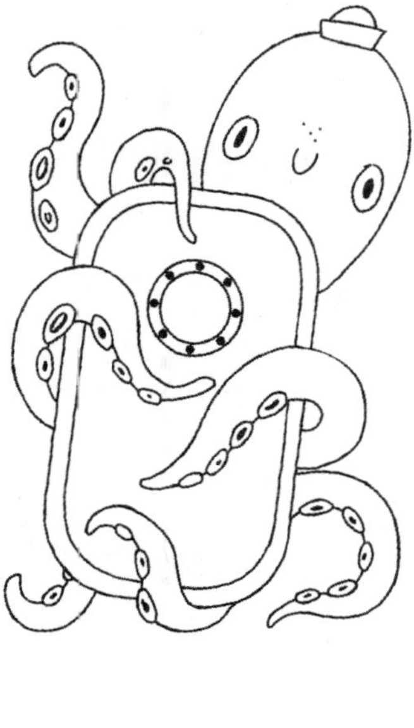

Knock, knock ...

Who's there?

Yul ...

Yul who?

Yul see when you open the door!

Knock, knock ...

Who's there?

Moo.

Moo who?

Well, make up your mind, are you a cow or an owl?

KNOCK, KNOCK ...

Who's there?

PHILIP ...

Philip who?

PHILIP MY GLASS PLEASE, IT'S EMPTY!

Knock, knock ...

Who's there?

Butcher.

Butcher who?

Butcher didn't know it was me at the door, did you?

Knock, knock ...

Who's there?

Karl ...

Karl who?

I'll Karl by another day when you're feeling more friendly!

Knock, knock ...

Who's there?

Ella.

Ella who?

Ella-vator. Doesn't that give you a lift?

KNOCK, KNOCK ...

Who's there?

CARLO.

Carlo who?

CARLOAD OF JUNK!

Knock, knock ...

Who's there?

Athena ...

Athena who?

Athena alien land outside your house!

Knock, knock ...

Who's there?

Galway ...

Galway who?

Galway, your annoying me!

Knock, knock ...

Who's there?

Alex ...

Alex who?

Alex the questions round here!

KNOCK, KNOCK ...

Who's there?

ICON ...

Icon who?

ICON TELL YOU A DIFFERENT KNOCK, KNOCK JOKE IF YOU LIKE!

Knock, knock ...

Who's there?

Button ...

Button who?

Button in is not polite!

Knock, knock ...

Who's there?

Fozzie ...

Fozzie who?

Fozzie hundredth time let me in!

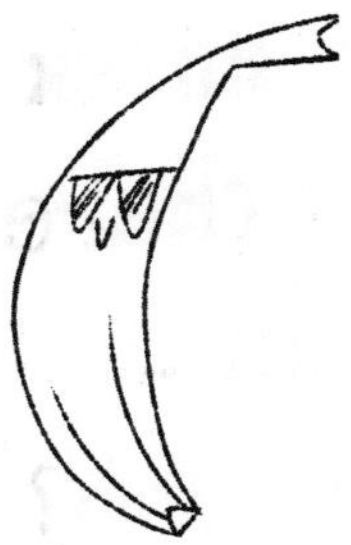

Knock, knock ...

Who's there?

Cole.

Cole who?

Cole as a cucumber!

Knock, knock ...

Who's there?

Spider.

Spider who?

Spider what everyone says, I like you!

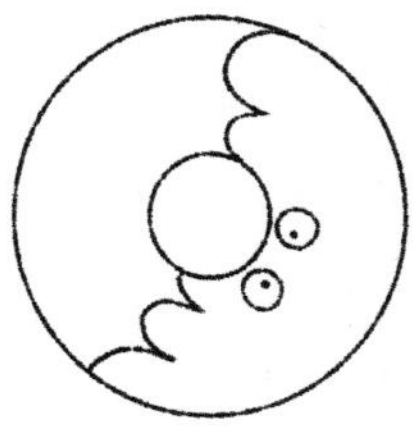

Knock, knock ...

Who's there?

Björn.

Björn who?

Björn to be wild!

KNOCK, KNOCK ...

Who's there?

WOODY ...

Woody who?

WOODY OPEN THE DOOR IF I ASK NICELY?

Knock, knock ...

Who's there?

Urchin ...

Urchin who?

Urchin has food on it!

Knock, knock ...

Who's there?

Mickey ...

Mickey who?

Mickey fell down the drain— do you have a spare?

Knock, knock ...

Who's there?

Jethro ...

Jethro who?

Jethro the key out of the window and I'll let myself in!

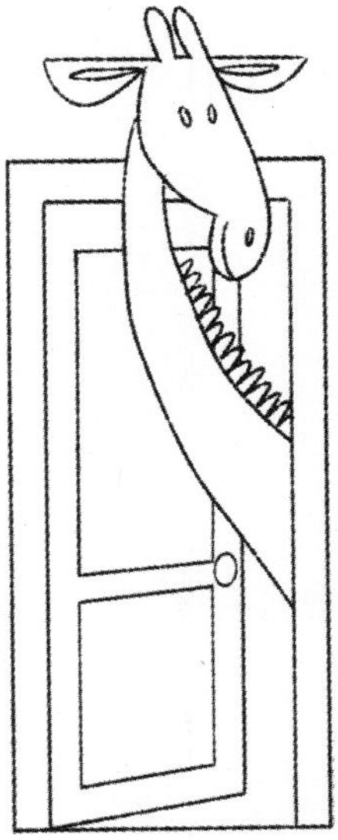

Knock, knock ...

Who's there?

Wanda ...

Wanda who?

Wanda know how much longer you're going to keep me waiting!

Knock, knock ...

Who's there?

May ...

May who?

Maybe its your best friend at the door!

KNOCK, KNOCK ...

Who's there?

ICING ...

Icing who?

ICING CAROLS THEN YOU GIVE ME MONEY!

Knock, knock ...

Who's there?

Juno ...

Juno who?

Juno what the time is, please?

Knock, knock ...

Who's there?

Ivana ...

Ivana who?

Ivana be inside!

Knock, knock ...

Who's there?

Meg ...

Meg who?

Meg up
your mind!

Knock, knock ...

Who's there?

Jupiter ...

Jupiter who?

Jupiter spaceship
on my lawn?

Knock, knock ...

Who's there?

Conyers.

Conyers who?

Conyers please
open the door!

KNOCK, KNOCK ...

Who's there?

OTTO ...

Otto who?

OTTOLD YOU WHO A MINUTE AGO!

Knock, knock ...

Who's there?

Izzy ...

Izzy who?

Izzy come, Izzy go!

Knock, knock ...

Who's there?

Julia ...

Julia who?

Julia want to come for a run with me?

Knock, knock ...

Who's there?

Dino ...

Dino who?

Dino what you're having for supper—I can smell it from here!

Knock, knock ...

Who's there?

Hayden ...

Hayden who?

Hayden seek.

Knock, knock ...

Who's there?

Cash ...

Cash who?

No, thanks. I prefer walnuts.

Knock, knock ...

Who's there?

Midas ...

Midas who?

Midas well open the door!

Knock, knock ...

Who's there?

Gin.

Gin who?

Gin know how cold it is out here today?

Knock, knock ...

Who's there?

Zeke ...

Zeke who?

Zeke and you shall find ...

Knock, knock ...

Who's there?

Alma ...

Alma who?

Alma-ny knock, knock jokes can you take?

KNOCK, KNOCK ...

Who's there?

CHOPIN.

Chopin who?

CHOPIN IN THE SUPERMARKET.

Knock, knock ...

Who's there?

Ahab.

Ahab who?

Ahab to go to the bathroom. Quick, open the door!

KNOCK, KNOCK ...

Who's there?

JESS ...

Jess who?

I GIVE UP, WHO?

Knock, knock ...

Who's there?

Noah ...

Noah who?

Noah don't know who you are either!

Knock, knock ...

Who's there?

Yul ...

Yul who?

Yuletide greetings to you and your kin!

Knock, knock ...

Who's there?

Osborn ...

Osborn who?

Osborn today—it's my birthday!

Knock, knock ...

Who's there?

Mikey ...

Mikey who?

Mikey won't fit in this lock!

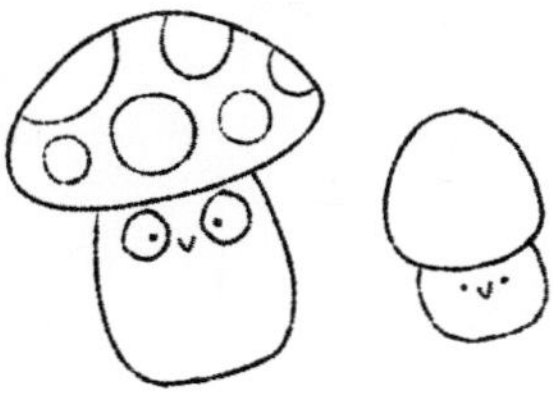

Knock, knock ...

Who's there?

Wade ...

Wade who?

Wade a minute, I'll just check!

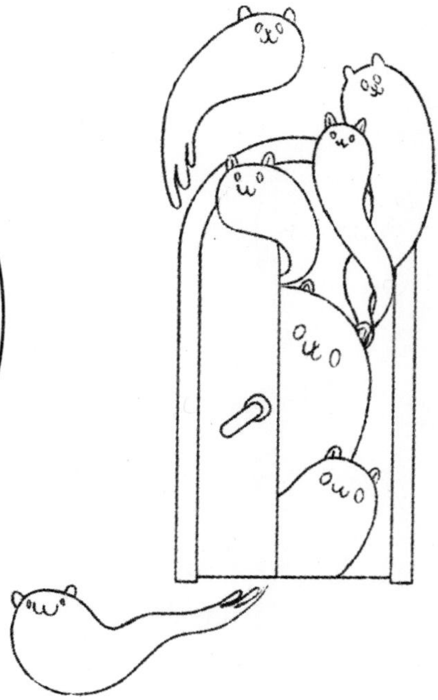

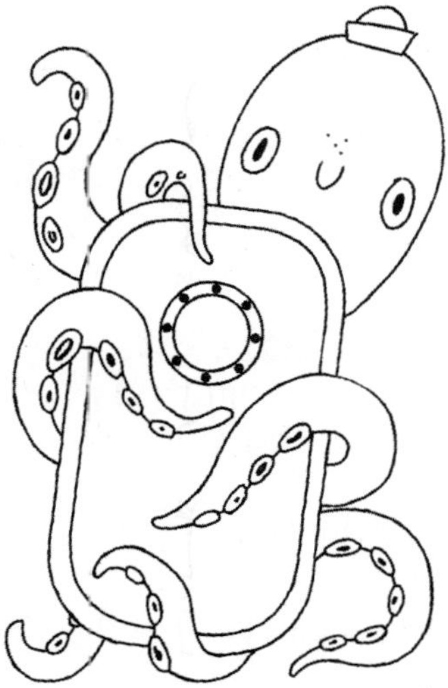

Knock, knock ...

Who's there?

Walter ...

Walter who?

Walter strange thing to ask!

Knock, knock ...

Who's there?

Hardy ...

Hardy who?

Hardy har, fooled you!

Knock, knock...

Who's there?

Freddie ...

Freddie who?

Freddie or not, here I come!

KNOCK, KNOCK ...

Who's there?

DENISE ...

Denise who?

DENISE ARE COLD— LET ME IN!

Knock, knock ...

Who's there?

Jaffa ...

Jaffa who?

Jaffa keep me waiting?

Knock, knock ...

Who's there?

Fangs.

Fangs who?

Fangs for the memory!

KNOCK, KNOCK ...

Who's there?

EARS ...

Ears who?

EARS LOOKING AT YOU!

Knock, knock ...

Who's there?

Butch ...

Butch who?

Butch your shoes on and come out here!

Knock, knock ...

Who's there?

Handsome ...

Handsome who?

Handsome chips to me and I'll tell you more!

KNOCK, KNOCK ...

Who's there?

NANA ...

Nana who?

NANA YOUR BUSINESS!

Knock, knock ...

Who's there?

Lettuce ...

Lettuce who?

Lettuce in and you'll find out!

Knock, knock ...

Who's there?

Who ...

Who who?

Is there an echo in here?

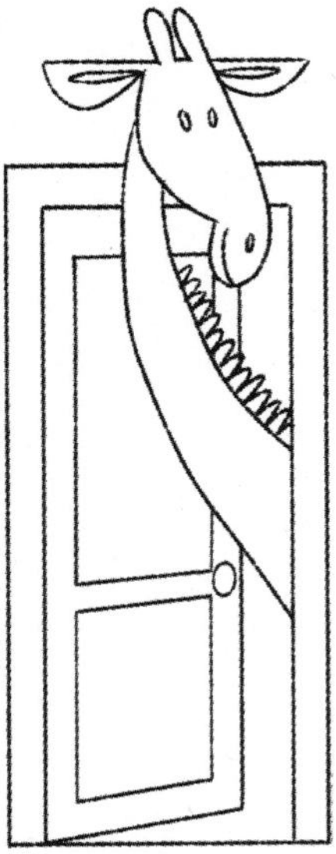

Knock, knock ...

Who's there?

Posy ...

Posy who?

Posy open the door and find out?

Knock, knock ...

Who's there?

Havelock ...

Havelock who?

Havelock put on your door!

Knock, knock ...

Who's there?

Genoa ...

Genoa who?

Genoa any new jokes? These are terrible!

Knock, knock ...

Who's there?

Rita.

Rita who?

Rita book, you might learn something!

Knock, knock ...

Who's there?

Jester ...

Jester who?

Jester minute, I'm trying to find my keys!

Knock, knock ...

Who's there?

Dwayne.

Dwayne who?

Dwayne the bathtub, it's overflowing!

KNOCK, KNOCK ...

Who's there?

MUFFIN ...

Muf n who?

MUFFIN THE MATTER WITH ME, HOW ABOUT YOU?

Knock, knock ...

Who's there?

Russell ...

Russell who?

Russell up a hot drink, will you? It's freezing out here!

Knock, knock ...

Who's there?

Felix ...

Felix who?

Felix my ice cream, I'll lick his!

Knock, knock ...

Who's there?

Aba.

Aba who?

Aba'out turn. Quick march!

Knock, knock ...

Who's there?

Cherry.

Cherry who?

Cherry oh, see you later!

Knock, knock ...

Who's there?

Indy.

Indy who?

Indy hallway is some of my stuff, and I've come to get it!

Knock, knock ...

Who's there?

Beethoven.

Beethoven who?

Beethoven is too hot!

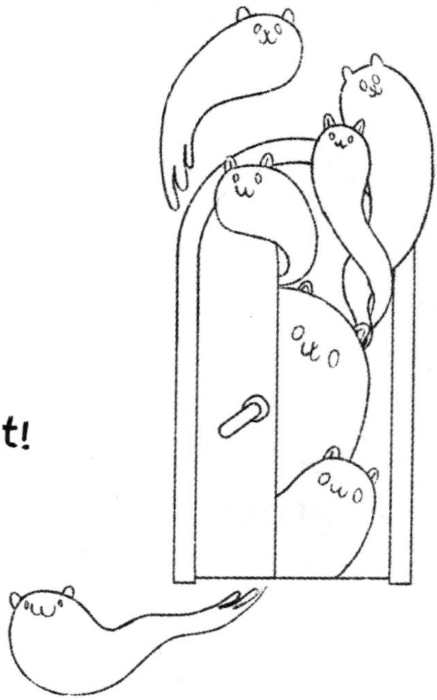

Knock, knock ...

Who's there?

Gordy.

Gordy who?

Gordy-rectly to jail, do not pass Go, do not collect da money!

Knock, knock ...

Who's there?

Bean.

Bean who?

Bean fishing lately?

Knock, knock ...

Who's there?

Carl ...

Carl who?

Carl get you there quicker than if you walk!

KNOCK, KNOCK ...

Who's there?

CAROL.

Carol who?

CAROL DOWN THE HILL, CALL THE POLICE!

Knock, knock ...

Who's there?

Greta ...

Greta who?

You Greta on my nerves!

Knock, knock ...

Who's there?

Olivia ...

Olivia who?

Olivia, but I lost my key!

Knock, knock ...

Who's there?

Florinda ...

Florinda who?

Florinda bathroom is wet, so be careful!

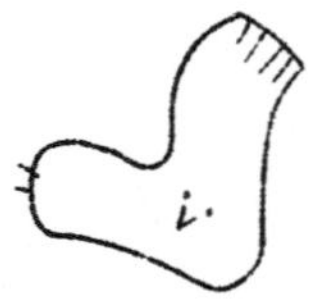

Knock, knock ...

Who's there?

Ferdie ...

Ferdie who?

Ferdie last time, open this door!

KNOCK, KNOCK ...

Who's there?

BABY ...

Baby who?

BABY I SHOULDN'T HAB COME ROUND WIV DIS COLD!

Knock, knock ...

Who's there?

Will ...

Will who?

Will wait out here until you let me in!

Knock, knock ...

Who's there?

Emma ...

Emma who?

Emma going to have to let myself in?

Knock, knock ...

Who's there?

JILLY ...

Jilly who?

**JILLY OUT HERE—
LET ME IN!**

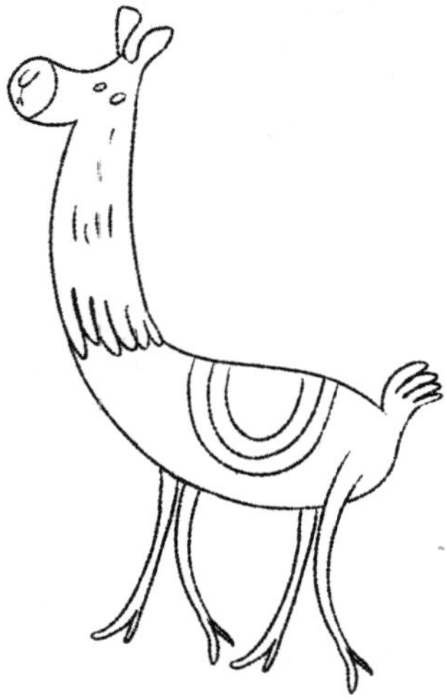

Knock, knock ...

Who's there?

Archie ...

Archie who?

Bless you!

Knock, knock ...

Who's there?

Bach ...

Bach who?

**Bach to work,
you slackers!**

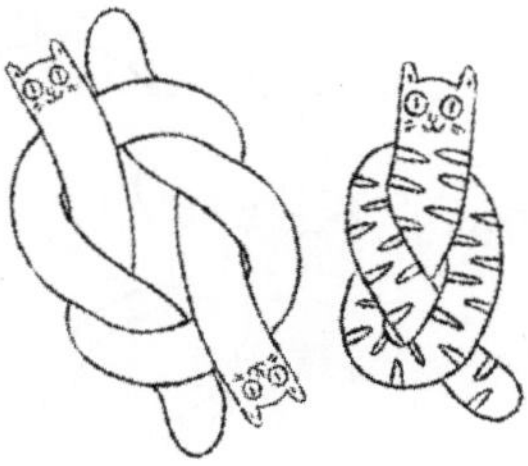

Knock, knock ...

Who's there?

Joan ...

Joan who?

Joan you remember me?

Knock, knock ...

Who's there?

Armageddon ...

Armageddon who?

Armageddon getting out of here!

KNOCK, KNOCK ...

Who's there?

BRAD ...

Brad who?

BRAD NEWS I'M AFRAID— YOUR DOORBELL'S BROKEN!

Knock, knock ...

Who's there?

Despair ...

Despair who?

Despair is flat, do you have a pump I could borrow?

Knock, knock ...

Who's there?

Fred ...

Fred who?

Fred you'll have to let me in!

KNOCK, KNOCK ...

Who's there?

MAY ...

May who?

MAY I come in?

Knock, knock ...

Who's there?

Adair ...

Adair who?

Adair once, but I'm bald now!

Knock, knock ...

Who's there?

Ellie.

Ellie who?

Ellie Funt.

Knock, knock ...

Who's there?

Posh ...

Posh who?

Posh the door open and you'll see!

Knock, knock ...

Who's there?

Les ...

Les who?

Les go for a swim!

Knock, knock ...

Who's there?

Pecan ...

Pecan who?

Pecan someone your own size!

Knock, knock ...

Who's there?

Esther ...

Esther who?

Esther anything I can do for you?

Knock, knock ...

Who's there?

Desi.

Desi who?

Designated hitter!

Knock, knock ...

Who's there?

Adolf ...

Adolf who?

Adolf ball hit me in de mouf!

Knock, knock ...

Who's there?

Figs ...

Figs who?

Figs the doorbell—my hand hurts from all the knocking!

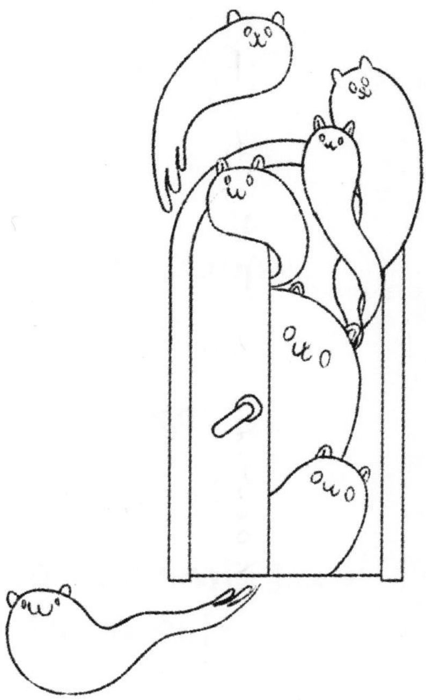

Knock, knock ...

Who's there?

Ya ...

Ya who?

What are you getting so excited about?

Knock, knock ...

Who's there?

Lena ...

Lena who?

Lena little closer and I'll tell you!

Knock, knock ...

Who's there?

Bart ...

Bart who?

Bart time you opened this door!

Knock, knock ...

Who's there?

Borg ...

Borg who?

Borg out of my mind!

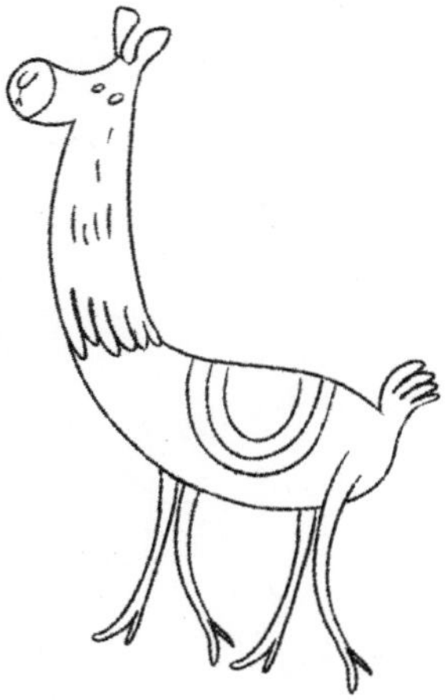

Knock, knock ...

Who's there?

Orange ...

Orange who?

Orange you glad to see me?

KNOCK, KNOCK ...

Who's there?

EUROPE ...

Europe who?

EUROPE TO NO GOOD!

KNOCK, KNOCK ...

Who's there?

LENNY ...

Lenny who?

LENNY IN, I'M HUNGRY!

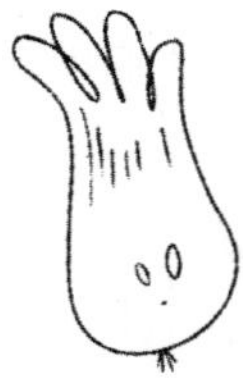

Knock, knock ...

Who's there?

Chester ...

Chester who?

Chester minute—I'm in the wrong street!

Knock, knock ...

Who's there?

Mike ...

Mike who?

Mike car has a flat—can I come in and use the phone?

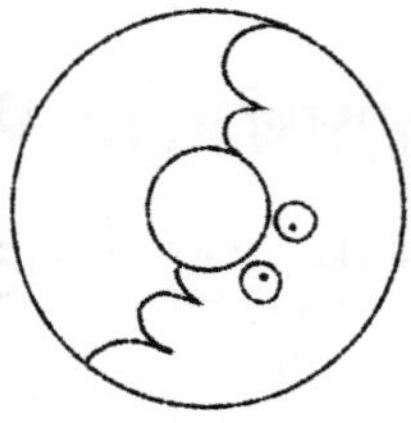

Knock, knock ...

Who's there?

Al ...

Al who?

Al give you a kiss if you open this door!

Knock, knock ...

Who's there?

Ear ...

Ear who?

Ear you are! I've been looking for you!

Knock, knock ...

Who's there?

Superman ...

Superman who?

You know I can't reveal my secret identity!

Knock, knock...

Who's there?

Leaf ...

Leaf who?

Leaf me alone!

Knock, knock ...

Who's there?

Essen ...

Essen who?

Essen it fun listening to these jokes?

Knock, knock ...

Who's there?

Ice cream ...

Ice cream who?

Ice cream every time I see a ghost!

KNOCK, KNOCK ...

Who's there?

VENICE.

Venice who?

VENICE THIS DOOR GOING TO OPEN?

Knock, knock ...

Who's there?

Lemon ...

Lemon who?

Lemon me give you a kiss!

Knock, knock ...

Who's there?

Alfie ...

Alfie who?

Alfie terrible if you leave!

CHAPTER 3

Crazy Jokes

KNOCK, KNOCK ...

Who's there?

BELLE ...

Belle who?

BELLE DON'T WORK, SO I HAVE TO KNOCK!

Knock, knock ...

Who's there?

Abbott ...

Abbott who?

Abbott time you opened this door!

Knock, knock ...

Who's there?

Phyllis ...

Phyllis who?

Phyllis up a glass of water!

Knock, knock ...

Who's there?

Sherlock ...

Sherlock who?

Sherlock your door or someone could break in.

Knock, knock ...

Who's there?

Butter ...

Butter who?

Butter open quick, I need the bathroom!

Knock, knock ...

Who's there?

Howell ...

Howell who?

Howell you have your pizza, plain or with pepperoni?

Knock, knock ...

Who's there?

Donna ...

Donna who?

Donna knock once more, then I'm going home!

Knock, knock ...

Who's there?

Giraffe ...

Giraffe who?

Giraffe to ask me that stupid question?

Knock, knock ...

Who's there?

Enid ...

Enid who?

Enid some more pocket money!

KNOCK, KNOCK ...

Who's there?

HOWARD.

Howard who?

HOWARD IS IT TO RECOGNIZE MY VOICE? I'M YOUR BEST FRIEND!

Knock, knock ...

Who's there?

Candice ...

Candice who?

Candice joke get any worse?

Knock, knock ...

Who's there?

Teresa ...

Teresa who?

Teresa jolly good fellow!

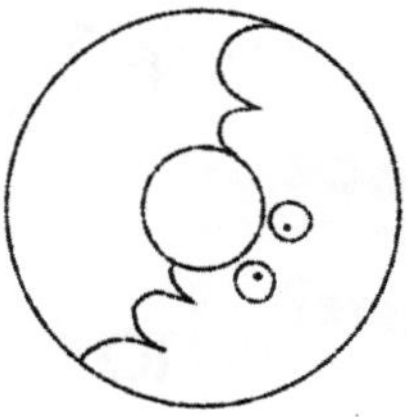

KNOCK, KNOCK ...

Who's there?

HUGO ...

Hugo who?

HUGO YOUR WAY AND I'LL GO MINE!

Knock knock ...

Who's there?

Police.

Police who?

Police can you stand still, I'm trying to take your photo!

Knock, knock ...

Who's there?

Arnie ...

Arnie who?

Arnie ever going to let me in?

Knock, knock ...

Who's there?

Eyesore ...

Eyesore who?

Eyesore do like you!

Knock, knock ...

Who's there?

You ...

You who?

Hello!

KNOCK, KNOCK ...

Who's there?

THAYER.

Thayer who?

THAYER THORRY OR I'LL THROW THITH PIE IN YOUR FACE!

Knock, knock ...

Who's there?

Ford.

Ford who?

Ford he's a jolly good fellow!

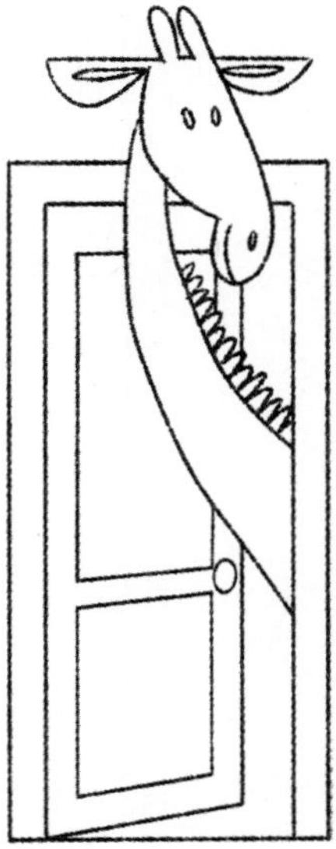

Knock, knock ...

Who's there?

Elsie ...

Elsie who?

Elsie you around!

Knock, knock ...

Who's there?

Scott.

Scott who?

Scott a creepy look about it, this place. I think it's haunted!

Knock, knock ...

Who's there?

Belize ...

Belize who?

Belize in yourself!

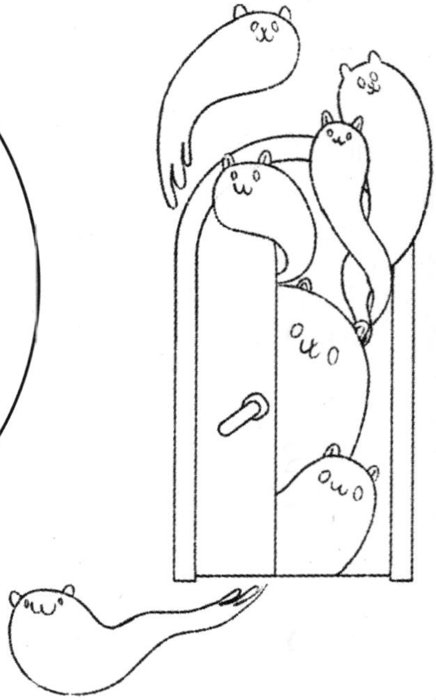

Knock, knock ...

Who's there?

Norma Lee ...

Norma Lee who?

Norma Lee I have my key, but today I left it at home.

Knock, knock ...

Who's there?

Batman ...

Batman who?

You mean there's more than one?

KNOCK, KNOCK ...

Who's there?

IKE ...

Ike who?

IKE COULD HAVE DANCED ALL NIGHT ...

Knock, knock ...

Who's there?

Abbey ...

Abbey who?

Abbey stung me on the nose!

Knock, knock ...

Who's there?

Andy.

Andy who?

Andy bee stung me again!

KNOCK, KNOCK ...

Who's there?

BACON ...

Bacon who?

BACON A CAKE FOR YOUR BIRTHDAY!

Knock, knock ...

Who's there?

Chaz ...

Chaz who?

Chaz pass the key through the window and I'll open the door myself!

Knock, knock ...

Who's there?

Sally ...

Sally who?

Sally-brate the best moments of your life!

Knock, knock ...

Who's there?

Lionel ...

Lionel who?

Lionel get you nowhere, you'd better tell the truth!

Knock, knock ...

Who's there?

Cassie.

Cassie who?

Cassie the wood for the trees!

Knock, knock ...

Who's there?

Ina ...

Ina who?

Ina minute I'm going to knock this door down!

Knock, knock...

Who's there?

Despair.

Despair who?

Despair room is full of junk!

Knock, knock ...

Who's there?

Barbara ...

Barbara who?

Barbara black sheep, have you any wool?

KNOCK, KNOCK ...

Who's there?

Ben ...

Ben who?

Ben knocking on this door all morning!

Knock, knock ...

Who's there?

Cello.

Cello who?

Cello, how are you?

Knock, knock ...

Who's there?

Nobel.

Nobel who?

Nobel, that's why I knocked!

Knock, knock ...

Who's there?

Hippo.

Hippo who?

Hippo-hop, dance till I drop!

Knock, knock ...

Who's there?

Mary ...

Mary who?

Mary Christmas, ho, ho, ho!

Knock, knock ...

Who's there?

Hannah.

Hannah who?

Hannah partridge in a pear tree!

Knock, knock ...

Who's there?

Rhoda.

Rhoda who?

Row, Row, Rhoda boat!

Knock, knock ...

Who's there?

Paul ...

Paul who?

Paul the door from your side—it's a bit stiff!

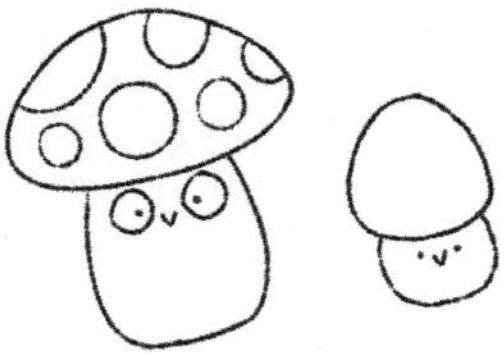

KNOCK, KNOCK ...

Who's there?

MARY LEE.

Mary Lee who?

MARY LEE, MARY LEE, LIFE IS BUT A DREAM! ROW, ROW ...

Knock, knock ...

Who's there?

Mike ...

Mike who?

Mike up your mind! Are you letting me in or not?

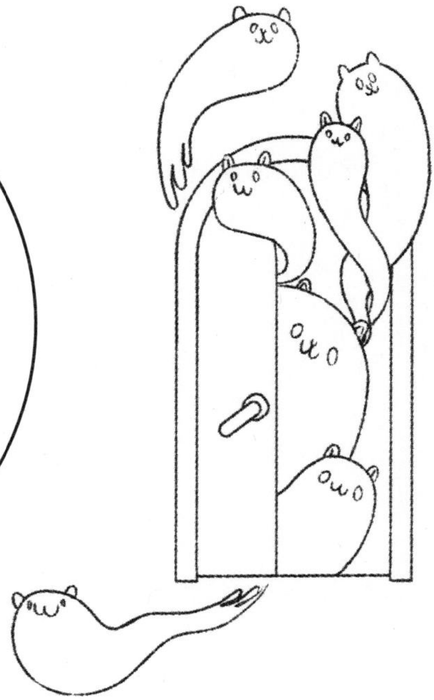

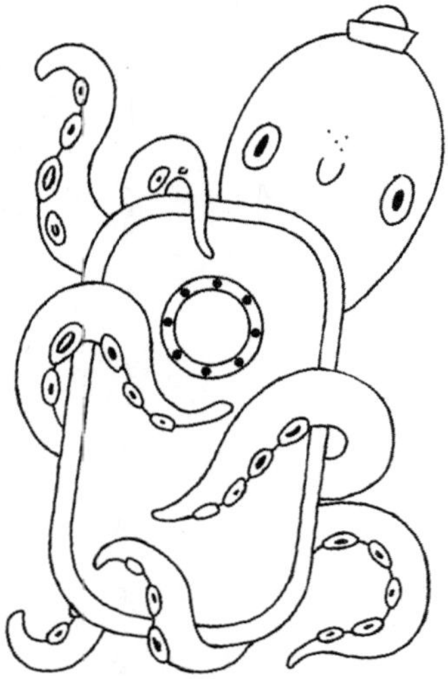

KNOCK, KNOCK ...

Who's there?

FOSTER ...

Foster who?

FOSTER THAN THE SPEED OF LIGHT!

Knock, knock ...

Who's there?

Polly ...

Polly who?

Polly door again, it's still stuck!

Knock, knock ...

Who's there?

Elias ...

Elias who?

Elias a terrible thing!

KNOCK, KNOCK ...

Who's there?

CHUCK ...

Chuck who?

CHUCK THE KEY UNDER THE DOOR AND I'LL LET MYSELF IN!

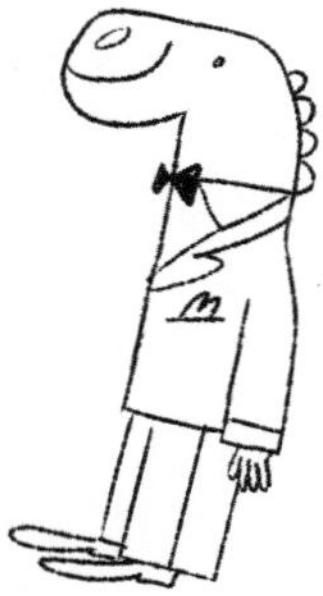

Knock, knock ...

Who's there?

Ali ...

Ali, who?

Ali-ttle old man who can't reach the doorbell!

Knock, knock ...

Who's there?

Eamonn ...

Eamonn who?

Eamonn a good mood today, so can I come in?

Knock, knock ...

Who's there?

Eddie ...

Eddie who?

Eddie body home?

Knock, knock ...

Who's there?

Barry.

Barry who?

Barry the treasure then no one will find it!

Knock, knock ...

Who's there?

Zookeeper.

Zookeeper who?

Zookeeper away from him!

Knock, knock ...

Who's there?

Argo.

Argo who?

Argo to dance class after school!

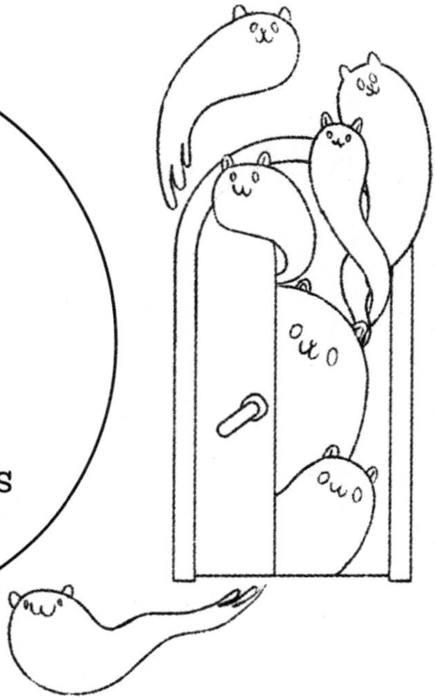

Knock, knock ...

Who's there?

Omar ...

Omar who?

Omar goodness gracious, I've got the wrong door!

KNOCK, KNOCK

Who's there?

KHAN

Khan who?

KHAN YOU GIVE ME A RIDE TO SCHOOL? I'M LATE!

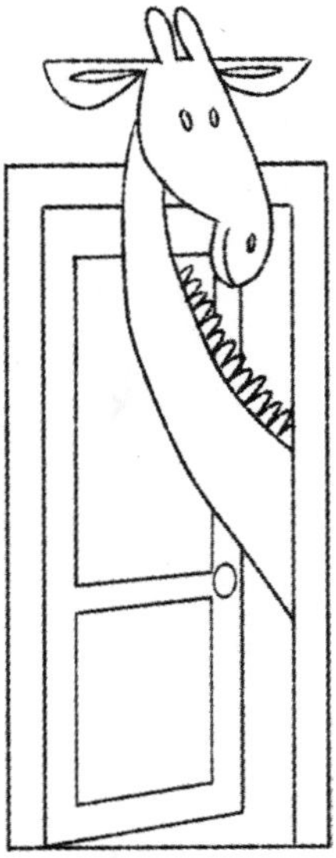

KNOCK, KNOCK ...

Who's there?

THEODORE ...

Theodore who?

THEODORE WASN'T OPEN SO I KNOCKED!

Knock, knock ...

Who's there?

Wendy ...

Wendy who?

Wendy red, red robin comes bob, bob bobbin' along, along ...

Knock, knock ...

Who's there?

Dummy ...

Dummy who?

Dummy a good deed and go away!

Knock, knock ...

Who's there?

Tessa ...

Tessa who?

Tessa long time for you to open the door!

Knock, knock ...

Who's there?

Arthur ...

Arthur who?

Arthur any more purple jelly beans in the jar? They're the best!

KNOCK, KNOCK ...

Who's there?

ZOMBIE.

Zombie who?

ZOMBIES MAKE HONEY, OTHERS ARE QUEENS!

Knock, knock ...

Who's there?

Charlie ...

Charlie who?

Charlie you know the sound of my voice by now!

Knock, knock ...

Who's there?

Buddha ...

Buddha who?

Buddha this slice of bread for me, will you?

Knock, knock ...

Who's there?

Zippy ...

Zippy who?

Zippy dee-doo-dah, zippy dee hey!

KNOCK, KNOCK ...

Who's there?

MABEL ...

Mabel who?

MABEL IS BROKEN TOO ...

Knock, knock ...

Who's there?

Usher ...

Usher who?

Usher wish you would let me in!

Knock, knock ...

Who's there?

Postman Pat.

Have you got a parcel?

No, but I've got a black and white cat!

Knock, knock ...

Who's there?

Eugene.

Eugene who?

Eugene, me Tarzan!

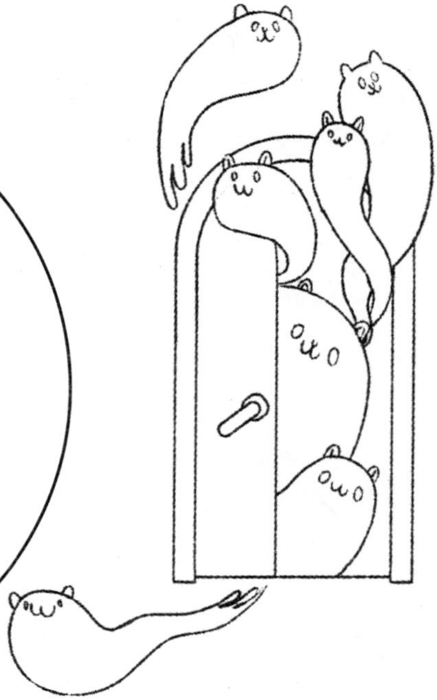

Knock, knock ...

Who's there?

Champ.

Champ who?

Champ-oo in my eyes. I can't see!

KNOCK, KNOCK ...

Who's there?

DAD.

Dad who?

DAD FUEL TO THE FIRE!

KNOCK, KNOCK ...

Who's there?

FARMER ...

Farmer who?

FARMER DISTANCE YOUR HOUSE LOOKS MUCH BIGGER!

Knock, knock ...

Who's there?

Carl ...

Carl who?

Carl my dad and ask him to come and pick me up!

Knock, knock ...

Who's there?

Sid ...

Sid who?

Sid down and I'll explain!

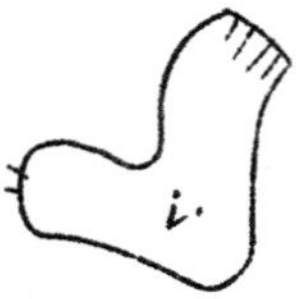

Knock, knock ...

Who's there?

Czech ...

Czech, who?

Czech who it is before you answer the door!

KNOCK, KNOCK ...

Who's there?

ELEMENT ...

Element who?

ELEMENT TO TELL YOU THAT SHE CAN'T COME ROUND TODAY.

Knock, knock ...

Who's there?

Courtney ...

Courtney who?

Courtney fish lately?

Knock, knock ...

Who's there?

Mandy ...

Mandy who?

Mandy lifeboats!

Knock, knock ...

Who's there?

Simon ...

Simon who?

Simon every occasion—youalways make me wait!

Knock, knock ...

Who's there?

Gary ...

Gary who?

Gary on smiling!

Knock, knock ...

Who's there?

Anna ...

Anna who?

Anna going to tell you, you'll have to keep guessing!

Knock, knock ...

Who's there?

Adelia ...

Adelia who?

Adelia the cards and we'll play snap!

Knock, knock ...

Who's there?

Brewster.

Brewster who?

Brewster wakes me up every morning singing cock-a-doodle-do!

Knock, knock ...

Who's there?

Annetta ...

Annetta who?

Annetta wisecrack and you're out of here!

KNOCK, KNOCK ...

Who's there?

DUNCE ...

Dunce who?

DUNCE-AY ANOTHER WORD!

Knock, knock ...

Who's there?

Handel.

Handel who?

Handel with care!

Knock, knock ...

Who's there?

Haydn.

Haydn who?

Haydn in this cupboard is boring!

KNOCK, KNOCK ...

Who's there?

CUSTER.

Custer who?

CUSTER LOT TO FIND OUT!

Knock, knock ...

Who's there?

Ada ...

Ada who?

Ada hot dog for lunch!

Knock, knock ...

Who's there?

Ray ...

Ray who?

Ray-ning cats and dogs.

Knock, knock ...

Who's there?

Phyllis ...

Phyllis who?

Phyllis bag with money, I'm a robber!

Knock, knock ...

Who's there?

Just Paul ...

Just Paul who?

Just Pauling your leg—it's me, not Paul!

Knock, knock ...

Who's there?

Yootha ...

Yootha who?

Yootha person with the bicycle for sale?

Knock, knock ...

Who's there?

Eye ...

Eye who?

Eye know who you are!

KNOCK, KNOCK ...

Who's there?

OLIVE ...

Olive who?

OLIVE NONE OF YOUR LIP!

Knock, knock ...

Who's there?

Henrietta.

Henrietta who?

Henrietta toadstool, but he thought it was a mushroom!

KNOCK, KNOCK ...

Who's there?

VIOLET ...

Violet who?

VIOLET THE CAT OUT OF THE BAG?

Knock, knock ...

Who's there?

Amanda.

Amanda who?

Amanda the table!

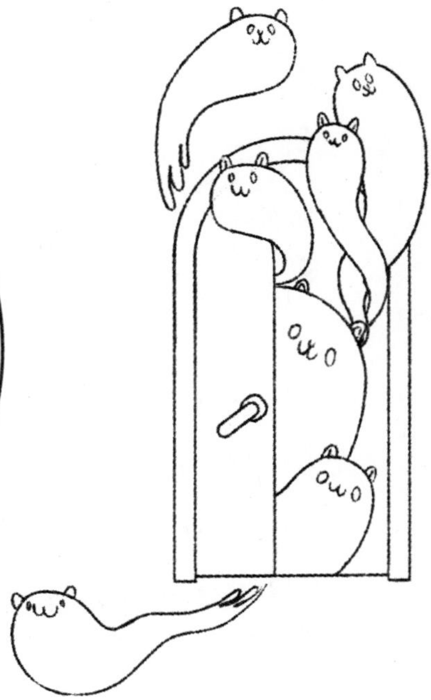

Knock, knock ...

Who's there?

Soup.

Soup who?

Souperman!

Knock, knock ...

Who's there?

Butternut.

Butternut who?

Butternut squash the eggs!

Knock, knock ...

Who's there?

Omelet.

Omelet who?

Omelet smarter than I look!

KNOCK, KNOCK ...

Who's there?

FANNY ...

Fanny who?

FANNY BODY CALLS, I'M OUT.

Knock, knock ...

Who's there?

Rather ...

Rather who?

Rather not come in, actually.

Knock, knock ...

Who's there?

Ken ...

Ken who?

Ken you stop locking me out? This is the third time I've knocked!

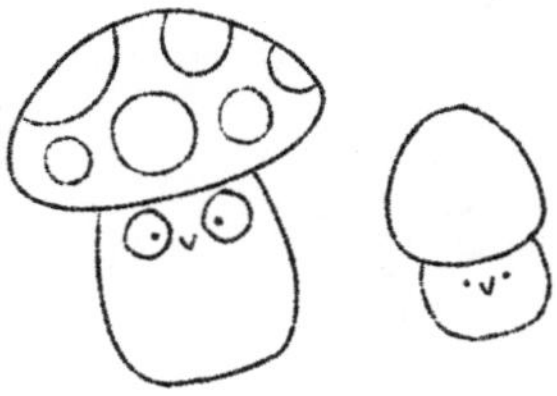

Knock, knock ...

Who's there?

Alexia ...

Alexia who?

Alexia again to open this door!

Knock, knock ...

Who's there?

Paula ...

Paula who?

Paula up the door handle will you and let me in!

KNOCK, KNOCK ...

Who's there?

TEX ...

Tex who?

TEX YOU AGES TO OPEN THE DOOR!

Knock, knock ...

Who's there?

Egbert ...

Egbert who?

Egbert no bacon!

KNOCK, KNOCK ...

Who's there?

CARLA ...

Carla who?

CARLA CAB, WE'RE LEAVING!

Knock, knock ...

Who's there?

Hammond ...

Hammond who?

Hammond eggs for breakfast.

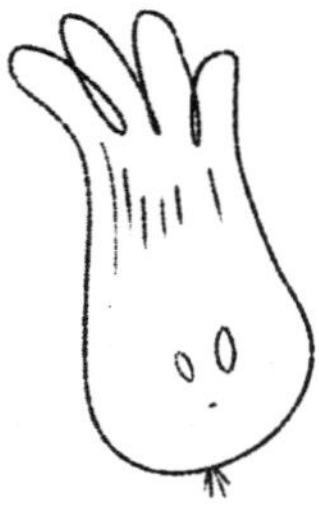

Knock, knock ...

Who's there?

Alpaca ...

Alpaca who?

Alpaca the big case, you pack the small one!

Knock, knock ...

Who's there?

Lucretia.

Lucretia who?

Lucretia from the Black Lagoon!

KNOCK, KNOCK ...

Who's there?

MARA.

Mara who?

MARA, MARA ON THE WALL!

Knock, knock ...

Who's there?

Aardvark ...

Aardvark who?

Aardvark a million miles for one of your smiles.

KNOCK, KNOCK ...

Who's there?

CECILE.

Cecile who?

CECILE TH-THE WINDOWS. TH-THERE'S A M-MONSTER OUT THERE.

Knock, knock ...

Who's there?

Pasture ...

Pasture who?

Pasture bedtime, isn't it?

Knock, knock ...

Who's there?

Yul ...

Yul who?

Yul see who when you open the door!

KNOCK, KNOCK ...

Who's there?

ALMA ...

Alma who?

ALMA NOT GOING TO TELL YOU!

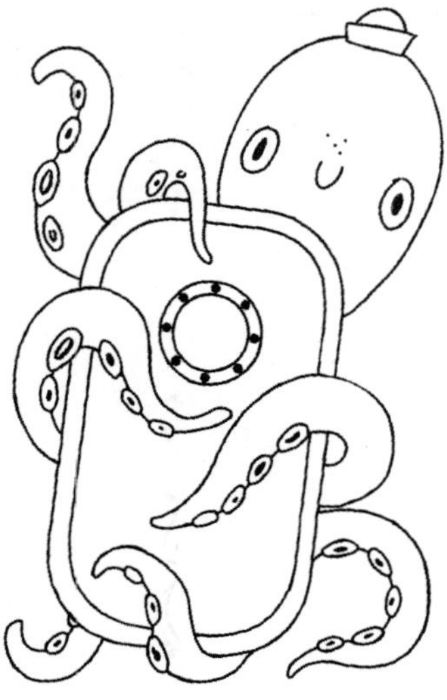

Knock, knock ...

Who's there?

Pizza.

Pizza who?

Pizza on Earth and goodwill to all men!

Knock, knock ...

Who's there?

Ozzie ...

Ozzie who?

Ozzie you still have the same front door as the last time I called!

Knock, knock ...

Who's there?

Radio ...

Radio who?

Radio not, here I come!

KNOCK, KNOCK ...

Who's there?

COOK ...

Cook who?

WHO ARE YOU CALLING CUCKOO?

CHAPTER 4

The Craziest Jokes

Knock, knock ...

Who's there?

Lionel ...

Lionel who?

Lionel get angry if you don't feed him!

Knock, knock ...

Who's there?

Sherwood ...

Sherwood who?

Sherwood like to meet you!

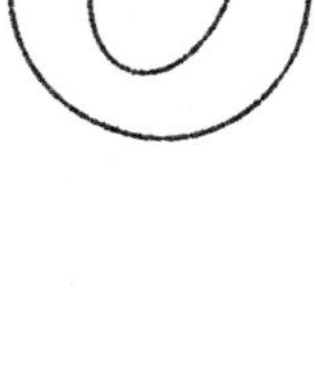

KNOCK, KNOCK ...

Who's there?

DIPLOMA.

Diploma who?

DIPLOMA TO FIX THE LEAK!

Knock, knock ...

Who's there?

Althea ...

Althea who?

Althea later, alligator!

Knock, knock ...

Who's there?

Lisa ...

Lisa who?

Lisa you can do is let me in!

Knock, knock ...

Who's there?

Spell ...

Spell who?

W ... H ... O!

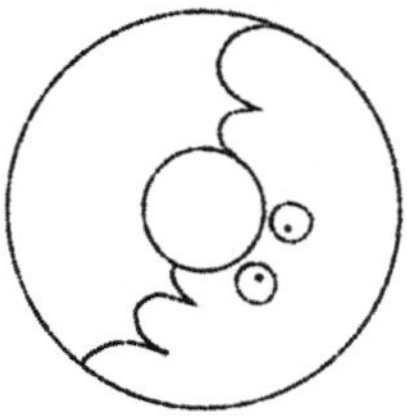

Knock, knock ...

Who's there?

Don Giovanni ...

Don Giovanni who?

Don Giovanni talk to me?

Knock, knock ...

Who's there?

Howard ...

Howard who?

Howard you know if you won't even open the door?

Knock, knock ...

Who's there?

Courtney ...

Courtney who?

Courtney door, can you open it and let me free?

Knock, knock ...

Who's there?

Congo ...

Congo who?

Congo out, I'm grounded!

Knock, knock ...

Who's there?

Alvin ...

Alvin who?

Alvin a great time, how about you?

KNOCK, KNOCK ...

Who's there?

SCOTT ...

Scott who?

SCOTT NOTHING TO DO WITH YOU!

Knock, knock ...

Who's there?

Boliva.

Boliva who?

Boliva me, I know what I'm talking about!

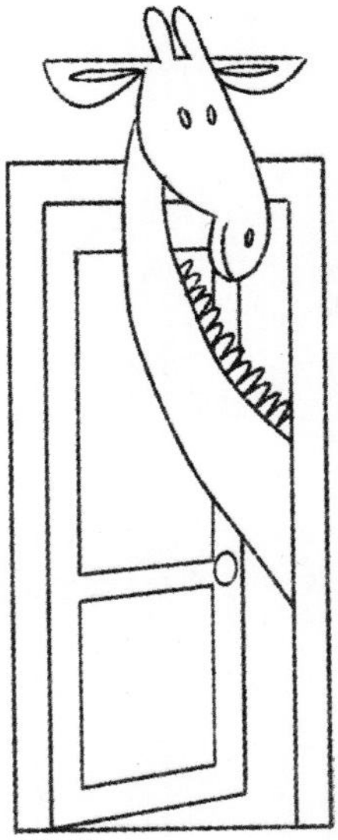

KNOCK, KNOCK ...

Who's there?

WILLA.

Willa who?

WILLA HURRY UP AND LET ME IN!

Knock, knock ...

Who's there?

Vera.

Vera who?

Vera long way from home and need a map!

Knock, knock ...

Who's there?

Value ...

Value who?

Value be my Valentine?

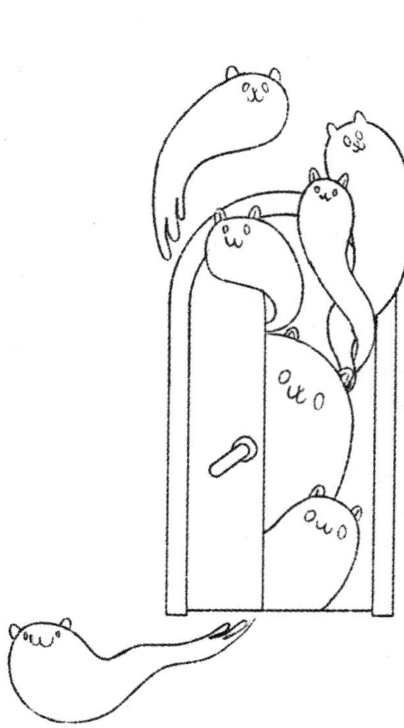

Knock, knock ...

Who's there?

Donna ...

Donna who?

Donna expect you to remember me, it's been a while!

KNOCK, KNOCK ...

Who's there?

VASSAR.

Vassar who?

VASSAR BOY LIKE YOU DOING IN A PLACE LIKE THIS?

KNOCK, KNOCK ...

Who's there?

SONIA.

Sonia who?

SONIA SHOE. I CAN SMELL IT FROM HERE.

Knock, knock ...

Who's there?

Munchin.

Munchin who?

Munchin my dinner and need a drink.

Knock, knock ...

Who's there?

Jack.

Jack who?

Jackpot! We've won first prize!

KNOCK, KNOCK ...

Who's there?

COHEN ...

Cohen who?

COHEN TO KNOCK JUST ONCE MORE, THEN I'M GOING TO GIVE UP!

Knock, knock ...

Who's there?

Donatello ...

Donatello who?

Donatello'n me!

Knock, knock ...

Who's there?

Deduct ...

Deduct who?

Donald Deduct!

Knock, knock ...

Who's there?

Dan ...

Dan who?

Dan just stand there—let me in!

Knock, knock ...

Who's there?

Dishes ...

Dishes who?

Dishes a very bad joke!

Knock, knock ...

Who's there?

Disk ...

Disk who?

Disk is a recorded message. Please leave your message after the beep!

Knock, knock ...

Who's there?

Bargain ...

Bargain who?

Bargain up the wrong tree!

Knock, knock ...

Who's there?

Diesel ...

Diesel who?

Diesel teach me to go around knocking on doors!

Knock, knock ...

Who's there?

Connor ...

Connor who?

Connor please open the door!

KNOCK, KNOCK ...

Who's there?

AMANA ...

Amana who?

AMANA BAD MOOD!

Knock, knock ...

Who's there?

Cam.

Cam who?

Camelot is where King Arthur lived!

Knock, knock ...

Who's there?

Colin ...

Colin who?

Colin in for a chat!

Knock, knock ...

Who's there?

Shelby.

Shelby who?

Shelby coming round the mountain when she comes!

Knock, knock ...

Who's there?

Olive.

Olive who?

Olive right next door to you!

Knock, knock ...

Who's there?

De Niro.

De Niro who?

De Niro I am to you, the more I like you!

Knock, knock ...

Who's there?

Imogen ...

Imogen who?

Imogenlifewithout chocolate!

Knock, knock ...

Who's there?

Water ...

Water who?

Water you doing in my house?

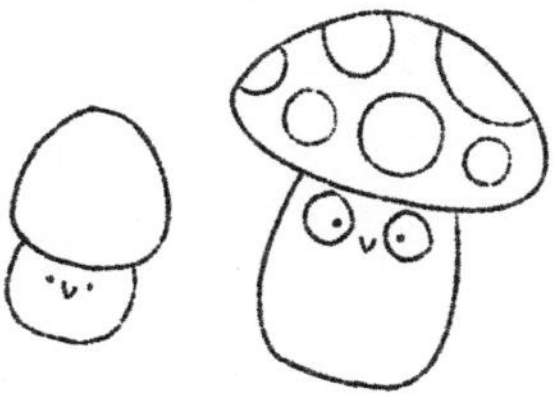

Knock, knock ...

Who's there?

Chicken ...

Chicken who?

Chicken the oven, I can smell burning!

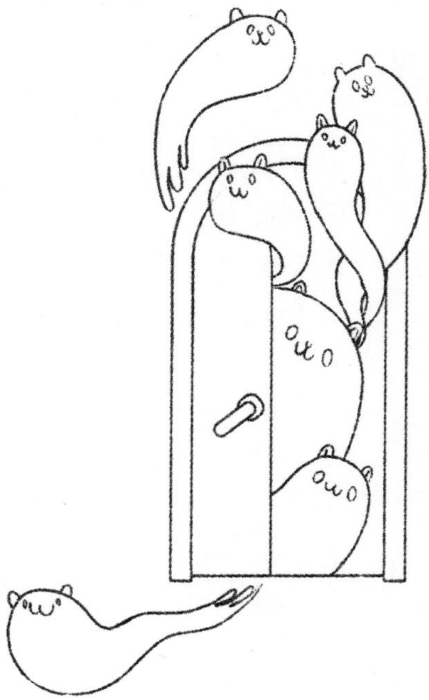

Knock, knock ...

Who's there?

Vince.

Vince who?

Vince some time since I saw you last!

Knock, knock ...

Who's there?

Jackson.

Jackson who?

Jackson the telephone, do you want to talk to him?

Knock, knock ...

Who's there?

Kay ...

Kay who?

Kay, L, M, N, O, P, Q, R, S, T, U, V, W, X, Y, Z!

KNOCK, KNOCK ...

Who's there?

OUR TELL.

Our Tell who?

OUR TELL YOU WHAT I WANT, WHAT I REALLY REALLY WANT!

Knock, knock ...

Who's there?

Heidi ...

Heidi who?

Heidi-Clare war on you!

Knock, knock ...

Who's there?

Ketchup ...

Ketchup who?

Ketchup with me and I will tell you.

Knock, knock ...

Who's there?

Joanna ...

Joanna who?

Joanna have a guess?

Knock, knock ...

Who's there?

Woody ...

Woody who?

Woody lend me some money for an ice cream, please?

KNOCK, KNOCK ...

Who's there?

BUTTER.

Butter who?

BUTTER BRING AN UMBRELLA, IT LOOKS LIKE IT MIGHT RAIN!

Knock, knock ...

Who's there?

Ivan ...

Ivan who?

Ivan idea you're going to keep me waiting out here a long time!

Knock, knock...

Who's there?

Rufus.

Rufus who?

Rufus on fire!

KNOCK, KNOCK ...

Who's there?

MCKEE ...

McKee who?

MCKEE DOESN'T FIT!

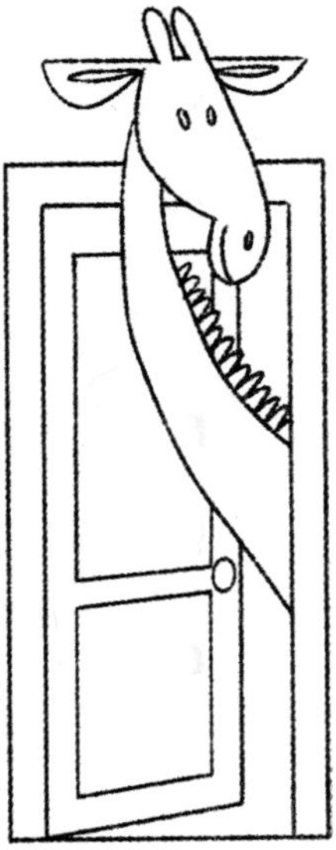

Knock, knock ...

Who's there?

Police.

Police who?

Police let me in, it's freezing out here!

KNOCK, KNOCK ...

Who's there?

MORSE.

Morse who?

MORSE COME IN AS QUICKLY AS POSSIBLE!

Knock, knock ...

Who's there?

Justin ...

Justin who?

Justin time to let me in!

KNOCK, KNOCK ...

Who's there?

WHOO OOO OOOO OOO ...

Whoo ooo oooo ooo who?

GREAT GHOST IMPRESSION!

Knock, knock ...

Who's there?

Thermos ...

Thermos who?

Thermos be a better knock, knock joke than this!

Knock, knock ...

Who's there?

Arch ...

Arch who?

You catching a cold?

Knock, knock ...

Who's there?

Banana ...

Banana who?

Knock, knock ...

Who's there?

Banana ...

Banana who?

Knock, knock ...

Who's there?

Banana ...

Banana who?

Knock, knock ...

Who's there?

Orange ...

Orange who?

Orange you glad I didn'tsaybanana?

Knock, knock ...

Who's there?

Deena ...

Deena who?

Deena hear me knock?

Knock, knock ...

Who's there?

Atlas ...

Atlas?

Atlas it's the weekend!

Knock, knock ...

Who's there?

Harry.

Harry who?

Harry you been?

Knock, knock ...

Who's there?

Mouse ...

Mouse who?

Mouse has burned down so I'm coming to stay with you!

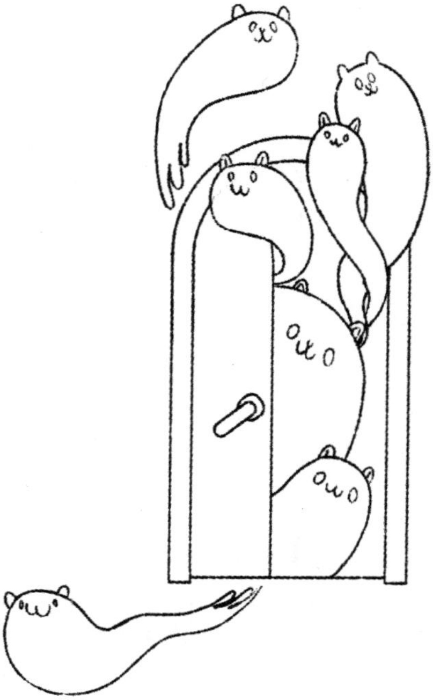

Knock, knock ...

Who's there?

Amos ...

Amos who?

Amos-quito is chasing me—please let me in!

Knock, knock ...

Who's there?

Pearce.

Pearce who?

Pearce this balloon with a pin!

KNOCK, KNOCK ...

Who's there?

ALFALFA.

Alfalfa who?

ALFALFA YOU, IF YOU GIVE ME A KISS!

KNOCK, KNOCK ...

Who's there?

IKE.

Ike who?

IKE CAN'T STOP LAUGHING!

Knock, knock ...

Who's there?

Lisbon.

Lisbon who?

Lisbon to see me, now she's come to see you!

Knock, knock ...

Who's there?

Wade.

Wade who?

Wade down upon the Swanee River!

Knock, knock ...

Who's there?

Avenue ...

Avenue who?

Avenueremembered you invited me for lunch?

Knock, knock ...

Who's there?

Gopher.

Gopher who?

Gopher broke!

KNOCK, KNOCK ...

Who's there?

ABBA, ABBA.

Abba, Abba who?

ABBA MERRY CHRISTMAS AND ABBA HAPPY NEW YEAR!

Knock, knock ...

Who's there?

Cyril ...

Cyril who?

Cyril nice to meet you!

KNOCK, KNOCK ...

Who's there?

ALISON.

Alison who?

ALISON AT THE KEYHOLE SOMETIMES!

Knock, knock ...

Who's there?

Guthrie.

Guthrie who?

Guthrie blind mice!

Knock, knock ...

Who's there?

Zeb ...

Zeb who?

Zeb better be a good reason for keeping me waiting out here!

KNOCK, KNOCK ...

Who's there?

ALEX ...

Alex who?

ALEX-PLAIN WHEN YOU OPEN THE DOOR!

Knock, knock ...

Who's there?

Callista.

Callista who?

Callista warm reception?

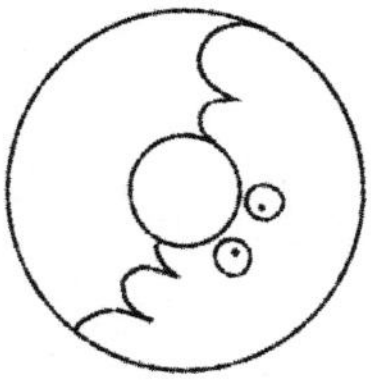

Knock, knock ...

Who's there?

Topic.

Topic who?

Topic a wild flower is against the law!

Knock, knock ...

Who's there?

Darren ...

Darren who?

Darren people in their flying machines!

KNOCK, KNOCK ...

Who's there?

WILLY.

Willy who?

WILLY LEND ME A STREET MAP? I'M A STRANGER IN TOWN!

Knock, knock ...

Who's there?

Sacha ...

Sacha who?

Sacha fuss, just because
I knocked on your door!

Knock, knock ...

Who's there?

Rosie.

Rosie who?

Rosie cheeks!

Knock, knock ...

Who's there?

Butter.

Butter who?

Butter let me in!

Knock, knock ...

Who's there?

A little girl ...

A little girl who?

A little girl who can't reach the doorbell!

Knock, knock ...

Who's there?

Olly ...

Olly who?

Olly need is love!

KNOCK, KNOCK ...

Who's there?

SID ...

Sid who?

SID YOU'D BE READY BY THREE—YOU'RE LATE!

Knock, knock ...

Who's there?

Josie ...

Josie who?

Josie anyone else out here?

KNOCK, KNOCK ...

Who's there?

AXL ...

Axl who?

AXL ME NICELY AND I MIGHT JUST TELL YOU!

Knock, knock ...

Who's there?

Etch ...

Etch who?

Bless you!

KNOCK, KNOCK ...

Who's there?

HOWL.

Howl who?

HOWL YOU KNOW UNLESS YOU OPEN THE DOOR?

Knock, knock ...

Who's there?

Steve.

Steve who?

Steveupperlip!

Knock, knock ...

Who's there?

Eeyore.

Eeyore who?

Eeyore-ways keeps me waiting!

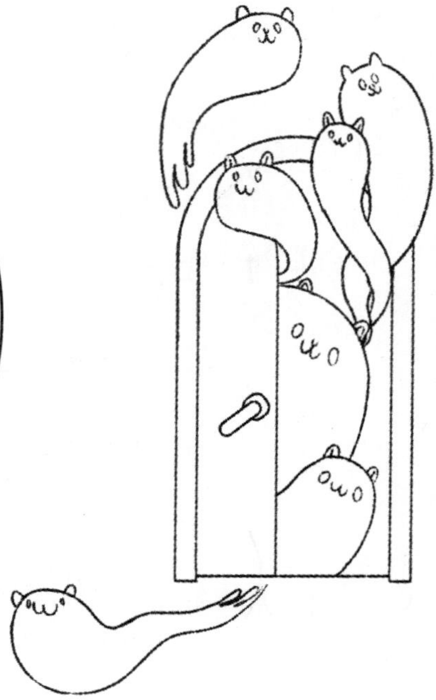

Knock, knock ...

Who's there?

Costas ...

Costas who?

Costas a fortune to get here.

Knock, knock ...

Who's there?

Alma ...

Alma who?

Alma time seems to be spent on this doorstep!

Knock, knock ...

Who's there?

Doris ...

Doris, who?

Doris locked, that's why I had to knock!

Knock, knock ...

Who's there?

Chad.

Chad who?

Chad to make your acquaintance!

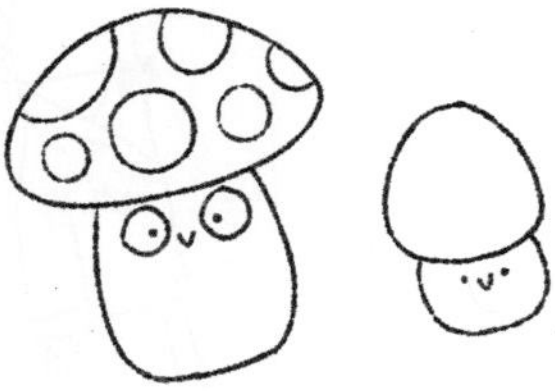

KNOCK, KNOCK ...

Who's there?

GORILLA ...

Gorilla who?

GORILLA CHEESE SANDWICH FOR ME AND I'LL BE RIGHT OVER.

Knock, knock ...

Who's there?

Cora.

Cora who?

Cora wish I had a door like this!

Knock, knock ...

Who's there?

Dennis.

Dennis who?

Dennisanyone?

Knock, knock ...

Who's there?

Chimney.

Chimney who?

Chimney cricket! Have you seen Pinocchio?

KNOCK, KNOCK ...

Who's there?

TEDDY.

Teddy who?

TEDDY IS THE BEGINNING OF THE REST OF YOUR LIFE!

Knock, knock ...

Who's there?

Jez.

Jez who?

Jez me, THAT'S WHO!

Knock, knock ...

Who's there?

U-8 ...

U-8 who?

U-8 my lunch!

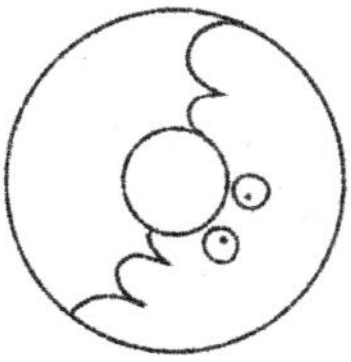

Knock, knock ...

Who's there?

Dragon.

Dragon who?

Dragon your feet again!

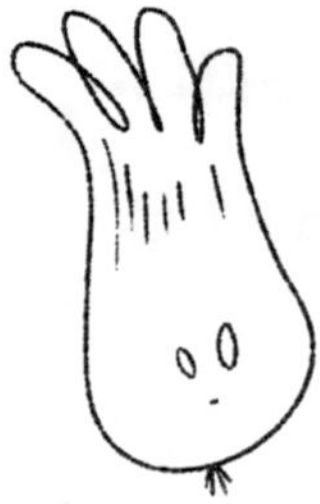

Knock, knock ...

Who's there?

Turkey.

Turkey who?

Turkey and find out!

KNOCK, KNOCK ...

Who's there?

FRESNO.

Fresno who?

RUDOLF THE FRESNO REINDEER!

Knock, knock ...

Who's there?

Avenue ...

Avenue who?

Avenue guessed yet?

Knock, knock ...

Who's there?

Annie ...

Annie who?

Annie one you like!

Knock, knock ...

Who's there?

Dublin.

Dublin who?

Dublin up with laughter!

Knock, knock ...

Who's there?

Rabbit ...

Rabbit who?

Rabbit up carefully, it's a gift!

Knock, knock ...

Who's there?

Ginger ...

Ginger who?

Ginger hear the doorbell?

KNOCK, KNOCK ...

Who's there?

YVETTE.

Yvette who?

YVETTE HELPS LOTS OF ANIMALS.

Knock, knock ...

Who's there?

Dale ...

Dale who?

Dale come if you ask dem!

KNOCK, KNOCK ...

Who's there?

BRIGHAM.

Brigham who?

BRIGHAM BACK MY SUNSHINE TO ME!

Knock, knock ...

Who's there?

Candace.

Candace who?

Candace be true?

Knock, knock ...

Who's there?

Yogurt.

Yogurt who?

Yogurt to love my jokes!

Knock, knock ...

Who's there?

Cozy ...

Cozy who?

Cozy who's knocking!

KNOCK, KNOCK ...

Who's there?

POLICE ...

Police who?

POLICE LET ME IN, IT'S COLD OUT HERE.

Knock, knock ...

Who's there?

Cynthia ...

Cynthia who?

Cynthiayoubeenaway I missed you!

Knock, Knock ...

Who's there?

Rock.

Rock who?

Rock-a-bye baby
on the treetop ...

KNOCK, KNOCK ...

Who's there?

WENDY ...

Wendy who?

**WENDY WIND BLOWS DE
CRADLE WILL ROCK ...**

Knock, knock ...

Who's there?

Donald ...

Donald who?

**Donald come baby,
cradle, and all ...**

CHAPTER 5

Very Funny Jokes

KNOCK, KNOCK ...

Who's there?

DEXTER ...

Dexter who?

DEXTER HALLS WITH BOUGHS OF HOLLY.

Knock, knock ...

Who's there?

Berlin ...

Berlin who?

Berlin the water to cook my eggs!

Knock, knock ...

Who's there?

Ben ...

Ben who?

Ben wondering what you've been up to!

KNOCK, KNOCK ...

Who's there?

BOO ...

Boo who?

DON'T CRY, IT'S ONLY A JOKE!

Knock, knock ...

Who's there?

Zone.

Zone who?

Zone shadow scares him!

Knock, knock ...

Who's there?

Cattle.

Cattle who?

Cattle purr if you stroke it!

Knock, knock ...

Who's there?

Jacklyn ...

Jacklyn who?

Jacklyn Hyde!

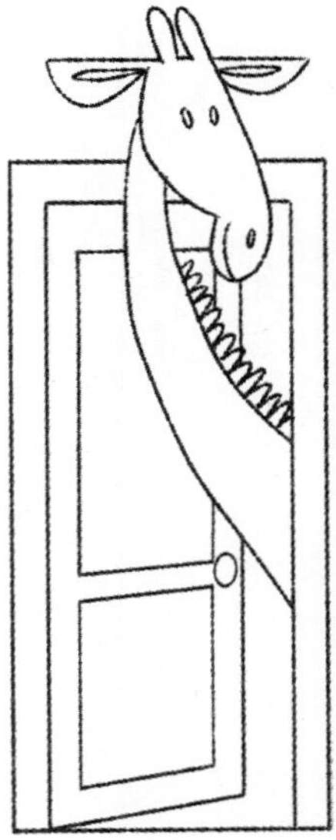

KNOCK, KNOCK ...

Who's there?

AUGUSTA.

Augusta who?

AUGUSTA WIND BLEW MY HAT AWAY!!

Knock, knock ...

Who's there?

Albee ...

Albee who?

Albee frozen if you leave me out here much longer!

Knock, knock ...

Who's there?

Veal chop.

Veal chop who?

Veal chop around and see vot bargains vee can pick up!

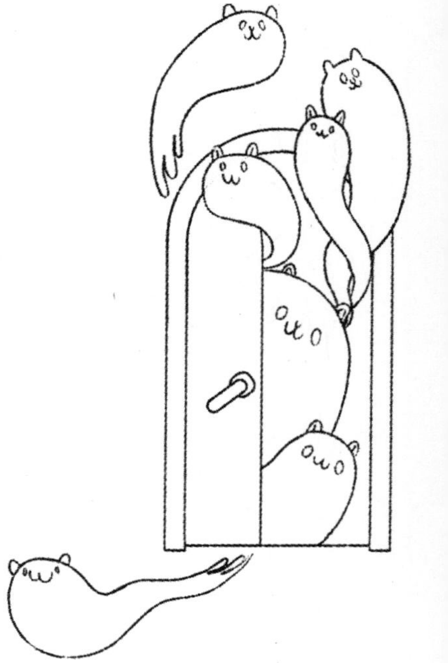

KNOCK, KNOCK ...

Who's there?

AMMONIA.

Ammonia who?

AMMONIA LITTLE KID!

Knock, knock ...

Who's there?

Cliff.

Cliff who?

Cliff hanger!

Knock, knock ...

Who's there?

Queen ...

Queen who?

Queen as a whistle!

Knock, knock ...

Who's there?

You are.

You are who?

I'm not who, I'm me!

Knock, knock ...

Who's there?

Canoe.

Canoe who?

Canoe come out and play today?

Knock, knock ...

Who's there?

Cy.

Cy who?

Cy'n on the dotted line!

KNOCK, KNOCK ...

Who's there?

DAKOTA.

Dakota who?

DAKOTA IS TOO SMALL!

Knock, knock ...

Who's there?

Derek.

Derek who?

Derek get richer and de poor get poorer!

Knock, knock ...

Who's there?

Major ...

Major who?

Major mind up whether you're going to open the door yet?

Knock, knock ...

Who's there?

Nobel ...

Nobel who?

Nobel, that's why I knocked!

KNOCK, KNOCK ...

Who's there?

OMAN ...

Oman who?

OMAN, YOU ARE CUTE!

Knock, knock ...

Who's there?

Colleen ...

Colleen who?

Colleen up this mess before I tell your parents!

Knock, knock ...

Who's there?

Theodore ...

Theodore who?

Theodore is stuck and it won't open!

KNOCK, KNOCK ...

Who's there?

CANDY ...

Candy who?

CANDY COW REALLY JUMP OVER DE MOON?

Knock, knock ...

Who's there?

Allied ...

Allied who?

Allied, I don't really want to come in!

Knock, knock ...

Who's there?

Cargo ...

Cargo who?

Cargo beep beep!

Knock, knock ...

Who's there?

Amy ...

Amy who?

Amy fraid I've forgotten!

KNOCK, KNOCK ...

Who's there?

ALDA ...

Alda who?

ALDA TIME YOU KNEW I WAS WAITING HERE!

Knock, knock ...

Who's there?

Japan ...

Japan who?

Japan is too hot! Ouch!

Knock, knock ...

Who's there?

Celeste ...

Celeste who?

Celeste time I'm going to ask—please can you let me in?

Knock, knock ...

Who's there?

Delores ...

Delores who?

Delores is on the side of the good guys!

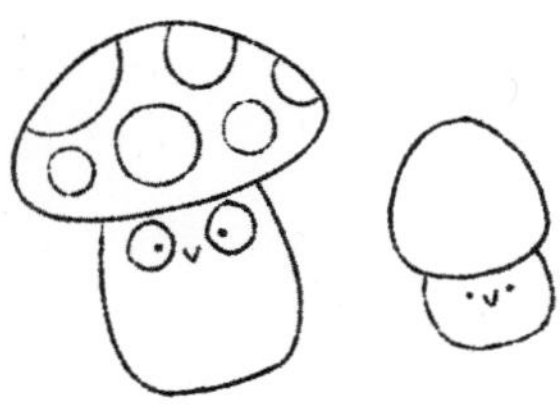

Knock, knock ...

Who's there?

Beezer.

Beezer who?

Beezer black and yellow and make honey!

Knock, knock

Who's there?

Lenny ...

Lenny who?

Lenny in, I'm HUNGRY!

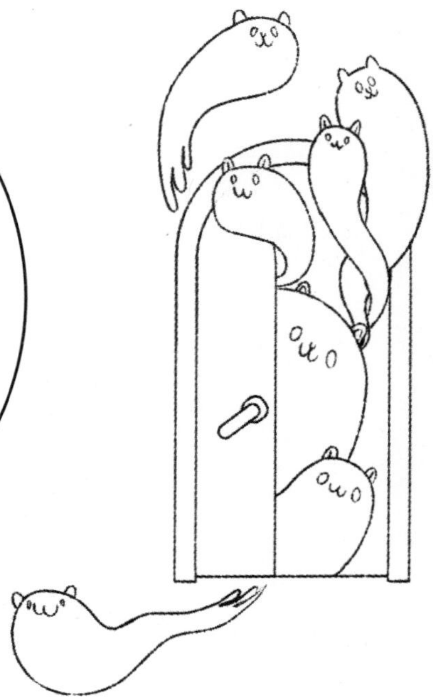

Knock, knock ...

Who's there?

Goose ...

Goose who?

Goose see a doctor, you don't look well!

Knock, knock ...

Who's there?

Alfred ...

Alfred who?

Alfred of the dark!

Knock, knock ...

Who's there?

Sarah.

Sarah who?

Sarah phone I can use?

KNOCK, KNOCK ...

Who's there?

DOCTOR ...

Doctor who?

NO, DOCTOR SMITH. I'M HERE TO SEE THE PATIENT ...

Knock, knock ...

Who's there?

Frank ...

Frank who?

Frankenstein. Arrrrgh!

Knock, knock ...

Who's there?

Jim ...

Jim who?

Jim mind if I stay here tonight?

KNOCK, KNOCK ...

Who's there?

YACHTS ...

Yachts who?

YACHTS UP, DOC?

Knock, knock ...

Who's there?

Chuck ...

Chuck who?

Chuck and see if the door is locked!

Knock, knock ...

Who's there?

Alien ...

Alien who?

Just how many aliens do you know?

Knock, knock ...

Who's there?

Pudding ...

Pudding who?

Pudding your shoes on before your pants is a bad idea!

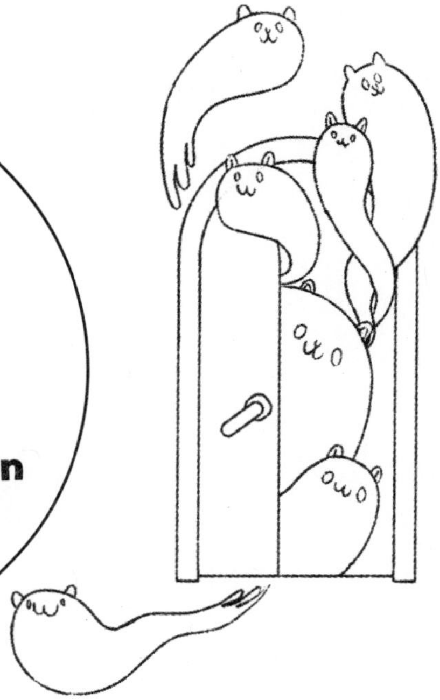

Knock, knock ...

Who's there?

Howard ...

Howard who?

Howard you like to be outside for a change!

Knock, knock ...

Who's there?

Constance.

Constance who?

Constance snoring is keeping me awake!

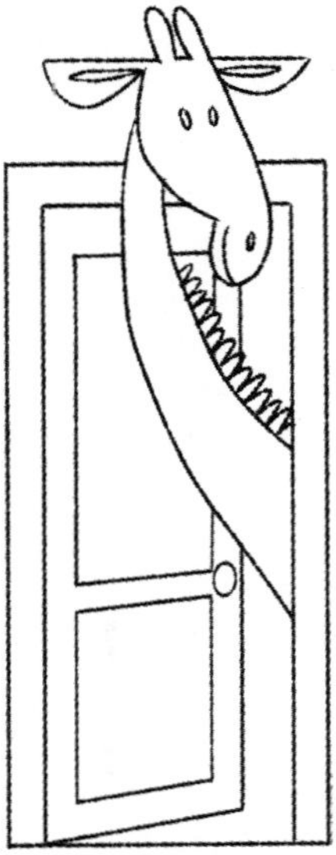

KNOCK, KNOCK ...

Who's there?

KEN ...

Ken who?

KEN YOU COME OUT TO PLAY?

Knock, knock ...

Who's there?

Juno.

Juno who?

Juno the answer?

Knock, knock ...

Who's there?

Yodel.

Yodel who?

Yodel who to you too! Let's form a yodelling duo!

Knock, knock ...

Who's there?

The Vampire.

The Vampire who?

The Vampire State Building!

Knock, knock ...

Who's there?

Max ...

Max who?

Max no difference to me!

Knock, knock ...

Who's there?

Chris.

Chris who?

Christmas is coming and the goose is getting fat!

KNOCK, KNOCK ...

Who's there?

ARMY.

Army who?

ARMY AUNTS COMING FOR DINNER?

Knock, knock ...

Who's there?

Ivor.

Ivor who?

Ivor sore hand from knocking!

Knock, knock ...

Who's there?

Hand.

Hand who?

Hand over your wallet, this is a raid!

Knock, knock ...

Who's there?

Jester.

Jester who?

Jester day, you were out. Today, you're in!

Knock, knock ...

Who's there?

Police ...

Police who?

Police stop telling these awful knock, knock jokes!

Knock, knock ...

Who's there?

Snow ...

Snow who?

Snow use—I can't remember!

Knock, knock ...

Who's there?

Carla ...

Carla who?

Carla restaurant, I'm hungry!

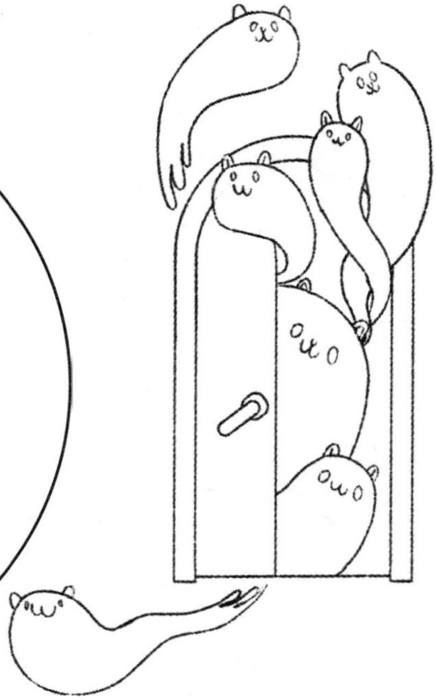

Knock, knock ...

Who's there?

Wood ...

Wood who?

Wood you like to let me in now?

Knock, knock ...

Who's there?

Hank ...

Hank who?

No, Hank you!

Knock, knock ...

Who's there?

Collier ...

Collier who?

Collier big brother then, see if I care!

Knock, knock ...

Who's there?

Pizza ...

Pizza who?

Pizza the pie!

Knock, knock ...

Who's there?

Ivan ...

Ivan who?

Ivan to come in, please open the door!

Knock, knock ...

Who's there?

Gladys ...

Gladys who?

Gladys the weekend, aren't you!

KNOCK, KNOCK ...

Who's there?

GOAT ...

Goat who?

GOAT TO THE DOOR AND FIND OUT!

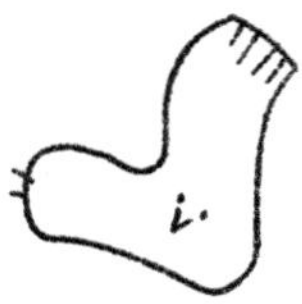

Knock, knock ...

Who's there?

Havana ...

Havana who?

Havana a great time. Wish you were here!

Knock, knock ...

Who's there?

Nuisance.

Nuisance who?

What's Nuisance yesterday?

Knock, knock ...

Who's there?

Holland ...

Holland who?

Holland you going to make me wait out here?

Knock, knock ...

Who's there?

Harriet.

Harriet who?

Harriet up!

Knock, knock ...

Who's there?

Arthur ...

Arthur who?

Arthur minute and I'll show you my identification!

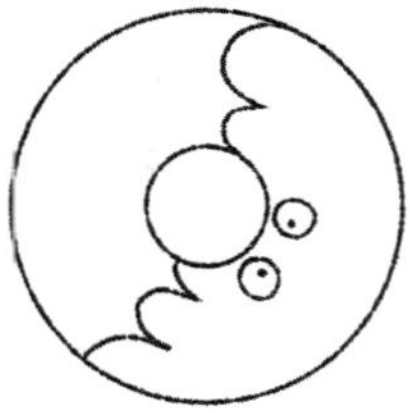

KNOCK, KNOCK ...

Who's there?

IRIS ...

Iris who?

IRIS YOU WERE HERE!

Knock, knock ...

Who's there?

Giraffe ...

Giraffe who?

Giraffe to sit right in front of me?

Knock, knock ...

Who's there?

Freighter.

Freighter who?

I'm Freighter open the door!

Knock, knock ...

Who's there?

Mayor ...

Mayor who?

Mayor come in?

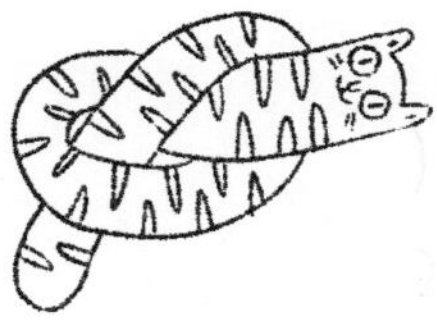

Knock, knock ...

Who's there?

Henrietta ...

Henrietta who?

Henrietta big dinner and now he feels sick!

Knock, knock ...

Who's there?

Zany ...

Zany who?

Zany body home?

KNOCK, KNOCK ...

Who's there?

DONUT ...

Donut who?

DONUT ASK, IT'S A SECRET!

Knock, knock ...

Who's there?

Kari.

Kari who?

Kari on like this and I'll freeze to death out here!

Knock, knock ...

Who's there?

Cecile ...

Cecile who?

Cecile this envelope!

Knock, knock ...

Who's there?

Isadore ...

Isadore who?

Isadore locked, I can't get in!

Knock, knock ...

Who's there?

Butcher ...

Butcher who?

Butcher money where your mouth is!

Knock, knock ...

Who's there?

C-2 ...

C-2 who?

C-2 it that you don't forget my name next time!

Knock, knock ...

Who's there?

Gandhi ...

Gandhi who?

Gandhi cane!

Knock, knock ...

Who's there?

Chris ...

Chris who?

Chris-p lettuce goes soggy if you leave it out!

Knock, knock ...

Who's there?

Anthem.

Anthem who?

Anthem prince seeking pretty princess.

KNOCK, KNOCK ...

Who's there?

ALBERT ...

Albert who?

ALBERT YOU DON'T KNOW WHO THIS IS!

Knock, knock ...

Who's there?

Watson ...

Watson who?

Watson TV tonight?

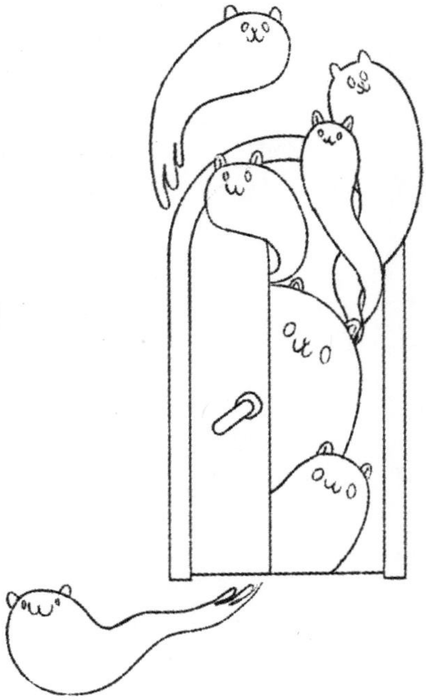

Knock, knock ...

Who's there?

Carmen ...

Carmen who?

Carmen get it!

Knock, knock ...

Who's there?

Glasgow ...

Glasgow who?

Glasgow to the movies!

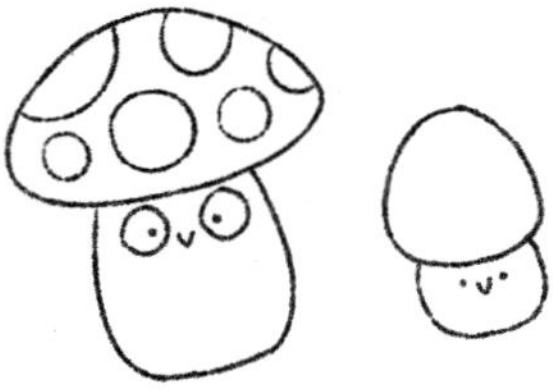

Knock, knock. ...

Who's there?

Mort ...

Mort who?

Mort to the point, who are you?

Knock, knock ...

Who's there?

Desiree.

Desiree who?

Desiree of sunshine in my life!

Knock, knock ...

Who's there?

Chester ...

Chester who?

Chester person delivering a parcel!

KNOCK, KNOCK ...

Who's there?

JETHRO ...

Jethro who?

JETHRO THE BOAT AND STOP TALKING SO MUCH!

Knock, knock ...

Who's there?

Bolton ...

Bolton who?

Bolton the door is stuck, can you try to undo it?

KNOCK, KNOCK ...

Who's there?

ALBEE.

Albee who?

ALBEE A MONKEY'S UNCLE!

Knock, knock ...

Who's there?

Diana.

Diana who?

Diana of thirst. Can I have a glass of water please?

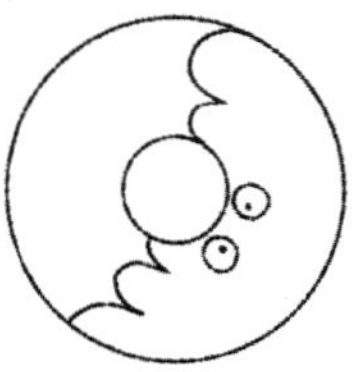

Knock, knock ...

Who's there?

Don Juan ...

Don Juan who?

Don Juan to go to school today!

Knock, knock ...

Who's there?

Dill.

Dill who?

Dill we meet again!

Knock, knock ...

Who's there?

Aida ...

Aida who?

Aida lot of cake and now I've got stomach ache!

Knock, knock ...

Who's there?

Alex ...

Alex who?

Alex to surf. What's your hobby?

Knock, knock ...

Who's there?

Zubin ...

Zubin who?

Zubin eating garlic again?

KNOCK, KNOCK ...

Who's there?

RUSSIA ...

Russia who?

RUSSIA WAY—THERE'S A MONSTER COMING!

Knock, knock ...

Who's there?

Leyland ...

Leyland who?

Leyland of the free and the home of the brave!

Knock, knock ...

Who's there?

Waddle ...

Waddle who?

Waddle you give me if I go away?

Knock, knock ...

Who's there?

Madrid ...

Madrid who?

Ma–drid you wash my jeans?

Knock, knock ...

Who's there?

Miniature ...

Miniature who?

Miniature open the door, I'll tell you!

Knock, knock ...

Who's there?

Ears ...

Ears who?

Ears some more knock, knock jokes for you!

KNOCK, KNOCK ...

Who's there?

HOMER ...

Homer who?

HOMER GOODNESS—I CAN'T REMEMBER MY NAME!

Knock, knock ...

Who's there?

Seymour ...

Seymour who?

Seymour of me by opening the door!

Knock, knock ...

Who's there?

Emma ...

Emma who?

Emma bit cold out here, can you let me in?

Knock, knock ...

Who's there?

Alva ...

Alva who?

Alva heart and let me in!

Knock, knock ...

Who's there?

Isabelle ...

Isabelle who?

Isabelle not working?

Knock, knock ...

Who's there?

Emmett ...

Emmett who?

Emmett your service!

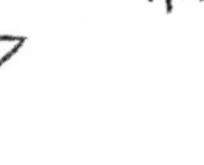

Knock, knock ...

Who's there?

Guess Simon ...

Guess Simon who?

Guess Simon the wrong doorstep!

Knock, knock ...

Who's there?

Fitz ...

Fitz who?

Fitz not too much trouble, can you please open the door?

KNOCK, KNOCK ...

Who's there?

MAE ...

Mae who?

MAE BE I'LL TELL YOU, OR MAE BE I WON'T ...

Knock, knock ...

Who's there?

Handsome.

Handsome who?

Handsome money through the keyhole and I'll tell you more!

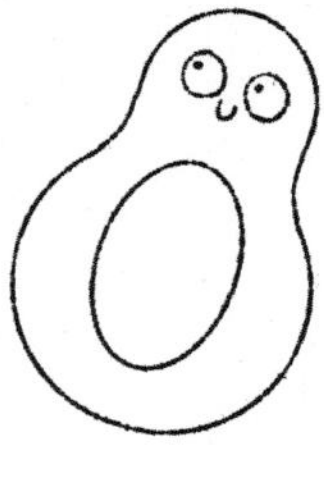

Knock, knock ...

Who's there?

Ben.

Ben who?

Ben down and tie your shoelaces!

Knock, knock ...

Who's there?

Duck.

Duck who?

Just duck—they're throwing things at us!

Knock, knock ...

Who's there?

Alec.

Alec who?

Alec-tricity. Isn't that a shock?

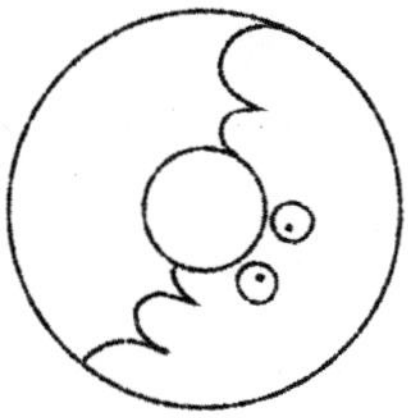

Knock, knock ...

Who's there?

Aki.

Aki who?

Aki would be really useful right now!

Knock, knock ...

Who's there?

Ethan.

Ethan who?

Ethan me out of house and home, you are!

Knock, knock ...

Who's there?

Teacher ...

Teacher who?

Teacher self for a few days, I'm having a break!

CHAPTER 6

Funniest Jokes of All

Knock, knock ...

Who's there?

Ella Man ...

Ella Man who?

Ella Man-tary my dear Watson!

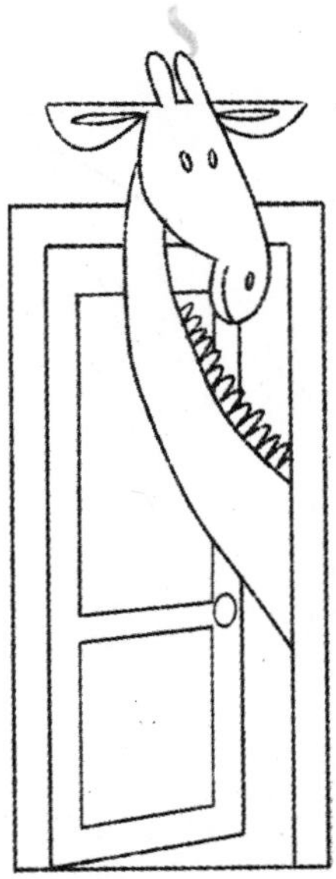

Knock, knock ...

Who's there?

Perth ...

Perth who?

Perth your lips and whistle!

Knock, knock ...

Who's there?

Haifa ...

Haifa who?

Haifa cake is better than none!

Knock, knock ...

Who's there?

Esau.

Esau who?

Esau you in the bath!

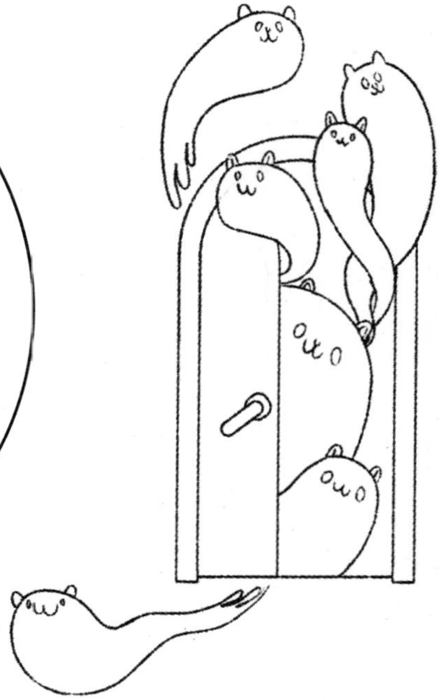

Knock, knock ...

Who's there?

I don't know ...

I don't know who?

I told you I don't know. Why don't you believe me?

Knock, knock ...

Who's there?

Spock ...

Spock who?

Spock the difference between me and my twin brother!

Knock, knock ...

Who's there?

Wendy.

Wendy who?

Wendy you want me to call round again?

Knock, knock ...

Who's there?

Arnie ...

Arnie who?

Arnie having fun?

KNOCK, KNOCK ...

Who's there?

TOFFEE.

Toffee who?

TOFFEE LOVED IS THE BEST FEELING IN THE WORLD!

Knock, knock ...

Who's there?

Sam ...

Sam who?

Sam person who knocked on the door last time!

Knock, knock ...

Who's there?

Earl ...

Earl who?

Earl be glad to tell you when you open this door!

Knock, knock ...

Who's there?

Scold ...

Scold who?

Scold out—let's go play in the snow!

KNOCK, KNOCK ...

Who's there?

TRIXIE ...

Trixie who?

TRIXIE COULDN'T DO BECAUSE HE WAS A BAD MAGICIAN!

Knock, knock ...

Who's there?

Haden.

Haden who?

Haden seek!

Knock, knock ...

Who's there?

Cass.

Cass who?

Cass more flies with honey than vinegar!

Knock, knock ...

Who's there?

Major ...

Major who?

Major headache—are there any painkillers?

Knock, knock ...

Who's there?

Dwayne ...

Dwayne who?

Dwayne in Spain falls mainly on the plain!

KNOCK, KNOCK ...

Who's there?

AHMED ...

Ahmed who?

AHMED A BIG MISTAKE COMING HERE!

KNOCK, KNOCK ...

Who's there?

KENT ...

Kent who?

KENT YOU STOP ASKING QUESTIONS AND JUST OPEN THE DOOR?

Knock, knock ...

Who's there?

Holly ...

Holly who?

Hollylujah!

Knock, knock ...

Who's there?

Kline ...

Kline who?

Kline of you to invite me round!

Knock, knock ...

Who's there?

Betty ...

Betty who?

Betty ya don't know who this is!

Knock, knock ...

Who's there?

Telly.

Telly who?

Telly your friend to come out!

Knock, knock ...

Who's there?

Olive.

Olive who?

Olive you!

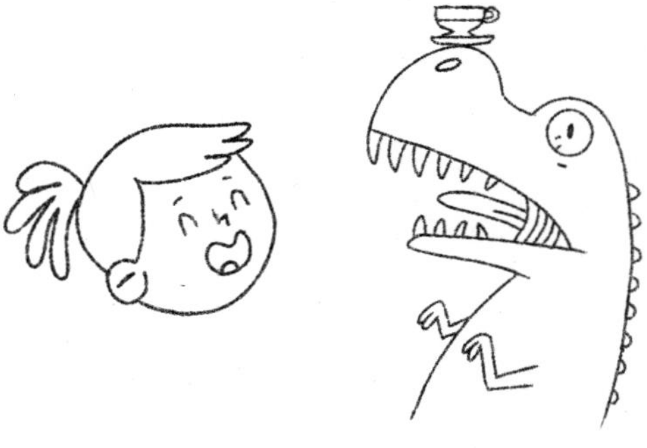

Knock, knock ...

Who's there?

Snow.

Snow who?

Snowbody here!

KNOCK, KNOCK ...

Who's there?

HOWARD ...

Howard who?

HOWARD CAN IT BE TO GUESS A KNOCK, KNOCK JOKE?

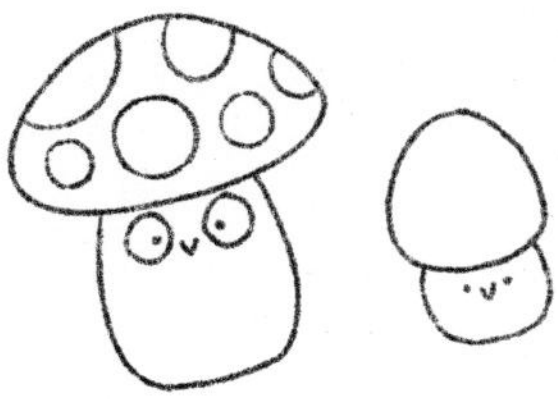

Knock, knock ...

Who's there?

Oink moo.

Oink moo who?

You are confused, aren't you?!

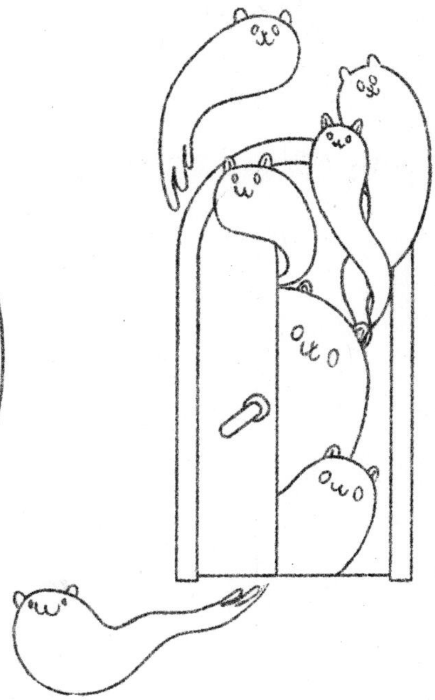

Knock, knock ...

Who's there?

Ben ...

Ben who?

Ben skiing lately?

KNOCK, KNOCK ...

Who's there?

DATSUN ...

Datsun who?

DATSUN OLD JOKE!

Knock, knock ...

Who's there?

Insurancesalesperson.

...

... hello ... ? hello ... ?

Knock, knock ...

Who's there?

Edwin.

Edwin who?

Edwin a cup if he could run faster!

Knock, knock ...

Who's there?

Amahl ...

Amahl who?

Amahl shook up!

Knock knock ...

Who's there?

Dishes ...

Dishes who?

Dishes me.

Knock, knock ...

Who's there?

Carol.

Carol who?

Carol go if you switch the ignition on!

Knock, knock ...

Who's there?

Jerrold ...

Jerrold who?

Jerrold friend, that's who!

Knock, knock ...

Who's there?

Ivan.

Ivan who?

Ivan infectious disease, so watch out!

Knock, knock ...

Who's there?

Ida ...

Ida who?

Ida bought a new doorbell when the last one broke!

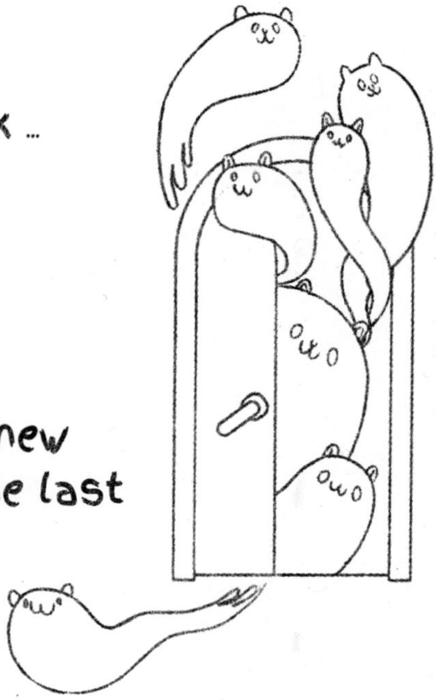

Knock, knock ...

Who's there?

Ooze ...

Ooze who?

Ooze in charge round here?

Knock, knock ...

Who's there?

Denise ...

Denise who?

Denise are above de ankles!

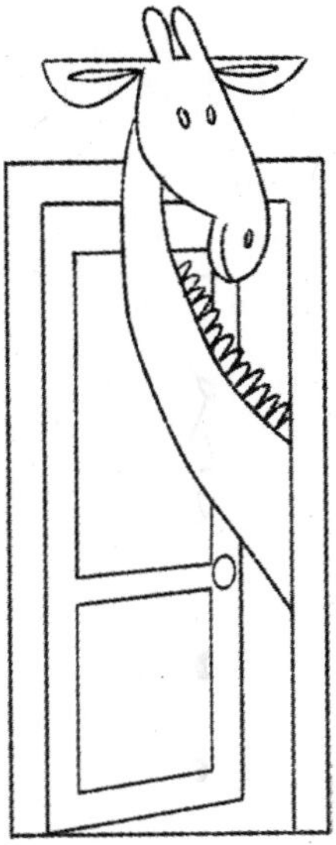

Knock, knock ...

Who's there?

Safari ...

Safari who?

Safari, so good...

Knock, knock ...

Who's there?

Lass ...

Lass who?

How long have you been a cowboy?

Knock, knock ...

Who's there?

Jerome ...

Jerome who?

Jerome at last!

Knock, knock ...

Who's there?

Ezra.

Ezra who?

Ezra no hope for me?

Knock, knock ...

Who's there?

Hedda ...

Hedda who?

Hedda nough of this—I'm off!

KNOCK, KNOCK ...

Who's there?

GWEN.

Gwen who?

GWEN ARE WE GOING TO GET TOGETHER?

Knock, knock ...

Who's there?

Ferrer.

Ferrer who?

Ferrer'vrything there is a season!

Knock, knock ...

Who's there?

Anita ...

Anita who?

Anita take the dog for a walk. Are you coming?

Knock, knock ...

Who's there?

Accordion ...

Accordion who?

Accordion to the weather forecast, it's going to rain tomorrow!

Knock, knock ...

Who's there?

Cows go ...

Cows go who?

No, cows go moo!

Knock, knock ...

Who's there?

Alfred ...

Alfred who?

Alfred the needle and you sew!

Knock, knock ...

Who's there?

ARF.

Arf who?

ARF FULL OR ARF EMPTY?

Knock, knock ...

Who's there?

Alaska ...

Alaska who?

Alaska the questions, not you!

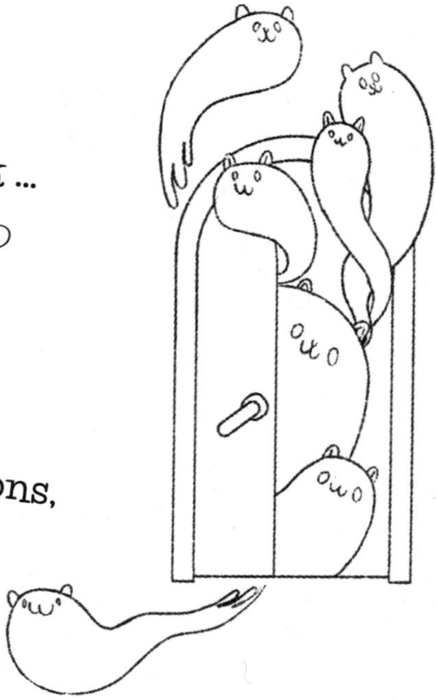

Knock, knock ...

Who's there?

Colin ...

Colin who?

Colin the doctor, I feel ill!

Knock, knock ...

Who's there?

Tuna.

Tuna who?

Tuna whole orchestra!

Knock, knock ...

Who's there?

Dozen ...

Dozen who?

Dozen anyone ever answer the door?

KNOCK, KNOCK ...

Who's there?

IKE ...

Ike who?

IKE-AN'T STOP LAUGHING!

Knock, knock ...

Who's there?

Tennis ...

Tennis who?

Tennis five plus five!

KNOCK, KNOCK ...

Who's there?

PAT.

Pat who?

PAT YOURSELF ON THE BACK!

Knock, knock ...

Who's there?

Red.

Red who?

Red your letters, you can have them back now!

Knock, knock ...

Who's there?

Butcher.

Butcher who?

Butcher said I could come and visit you!

Knock, knock.

Who's there?

Owls say.

Owls say who?

Yes, they do!

KNOCK, KNOCK ...

Who's there?

PARTON ...

Parton who?

PARTON MY FRENCH!

Knock, knock ...

Who's there?

Beets ...

Beets who?

Beets me!

Knock, knock ...

Who's there?

Annie ...

Annie who?

Annie thing you can do, I can do better.

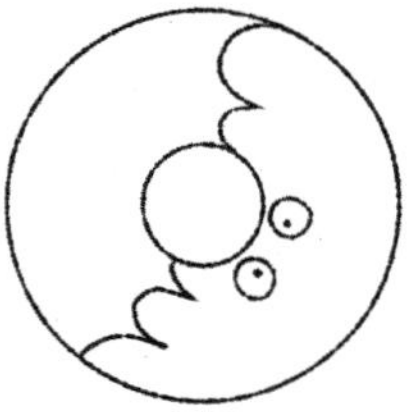

Knock, knock ...

Who's there?

Alaska.

Alaska who?

Alaska again, please open the door!

Knock, knock ...

Who's there?

Josie ...

Josie who?

Josie any reason to keep me waiting out here?

Knock, knock ...

Who's there?

Bertha ...

Bertha who?

Bertha-day greetings!

Knock, knock ...

Who's there?

Aretha.

Aretha who?

Aretha holly on your door.

Knock, knock ...

Who's there?

Formosa ...

Formosa who?

Formosa the summer I was away camping.

KNOCK, KNOCK ...

Who's there?

LUCK.

Luck who?

LUCK THROUGH THE KEYHOLE AND YOU'LL FIND OUT!

Knock, knock ...

Who's there?

Aaron ...

Aaron who?

Aaron on the side of caution!

Knock, knock ...

Who's there?

Amory.

Amory who?

Amory Christmas!

Knock Knock

Who's there?

Opportunity.

Stop being silly, opportunity only knocks once!

KNOCK, KNOCK ...

Who's there?

DON.

Don who?

DON BE AFRAID ... LOOK INTO MY EYES ... YOU ARE FEELING SLEEPY ...

Knock, knock ...

Who's there?

Suspense ...

Suspense who?

...

Knock, knock ...

Who's there?

Nadia ...

Nadia who?

Nadia head if you understand what I'm saying.

Knock, knock ...

Who's there?

I love ...

I love who?

I don't know, you tell me!

Knock, knock ...

Who's there?

Paula ...

Paula who?

Paula door open and you'll see!

KNOCK, KNOCK ...

Who's there?

TOM SAWYER.

Tom Sawyer who?

TOM SAWYER UNDERWEAR!

Knock, knock ...

Who's there?

Darwin.

Darwin who?

I'll be Darwin you open the door!

Knock, knock ...

Who's there?

Fletch ...

Fletch who?

Fletch the fire fighters, there's smoke coming from your window!

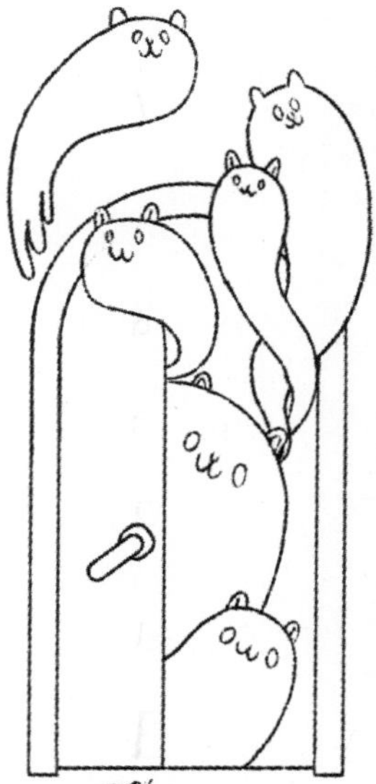

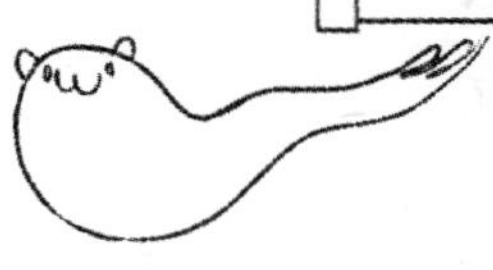

Knock, knock ...

Who's there?

Hawaii ...

Hawaii who?

I'm fine, Hawaii you?

Knock, knock ...

Who's there?

Honeybee ...

Honeybee who?

Honeybee a dear and open the door!

Knock, knock ...

Who's there?

Paul ...

Paul who?

Paul the door open for goodness sake!

Knock, knock ...

Who's there?

Greta ...

Greta who?

Greta friend like that again, and you'll end up with none at all!

Knock, knock ...

Who's there?

Edith.

Edith who?

Edith, it'll make you feel better!

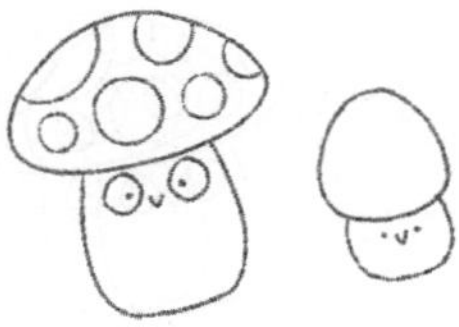

Knock, knock ...

Who's there?

Kanga ...

Kanga who?

No! Kanga roo!

Knock, knock ...

Who's there?

Lee King ...

Lee King who?

Lee King bucket. Can I borrow yours?

KNOCK, KNOCK ...

Who's there?

WENDY ...

Wendy who?

WENDY YOU WANT ME TO WALK YOUR DOG AGAIN?

Knock, knock ...

Who's there?

Candy ...

Candy who?

Candy owner of this big red car come and move it off my drive!

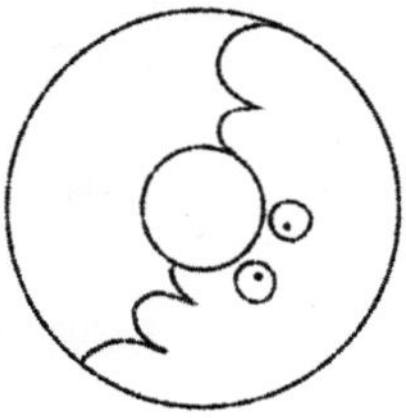

Knock, knock ...

Who's there?

Donalette.

Donalette who?

Donalette the bed bugs bite!

Knock, knock ...

Who's there?

Giselle ...

Giselle who?

Giselle flowers here, or have I got the wrong store?

Knock, knock ...

Who's there?

Passion ...

Passion who?

Passion through and thought I'd say hello!

Knock, knock ...

Who's there?

Waiter ...

Waiter who?

Waiter minute while I tie my shoelaces.

Knock, knock ...

Who's there?

Mustapha ...

Mustapha who?

Mustapha good reason to keep me waiting so long!

Knock, knock ...

Who's there?

Deanna ...

Deanna who?

Deanna-mals are restless, I think they need feeding!

KNOCK, KNOCK ...

Who's there?

I AM.

I am who?

YOU DON'T KNOW WHO YOU ARE?

Knock, knock ...

Who's there?

Honor Claire.

Honor Claire who?

Honor Claire day, you can see for miles!

Knock, knock ...

Who's there?

Anka.

Anka who?

Anka the ship!

Knock, knock ...

Who's there?

Daryl ...

Daryl who?

Daryl never be another you ...

Knock, knock ...

Who's there?

Hans.

Hans who?

Hans off the table!

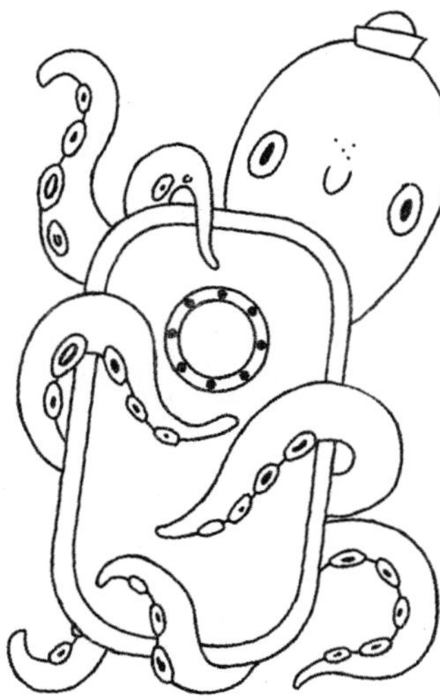

KNOCK, KNOCK ...

Who's there?

WILLY ...

Willy who?

WILLY LET ME USE YOUR WASHING MACHINE? MINE'S BROKEN!

Knock, knock ...

Who's there?

Douglas ...

Douglas who?

Douglas is broken in your front door!

Knock, knock ...

Who's there?

Dishes ...

Dishes who?

Dishes the life!

Knock, knock ...

Who's there?

Juicy ...

Juicy who?

Juicy what I just saw?

KNOCK, KNOCK ...

Who's there?

TURNER.

Turner who?

TURNER ROUND, THERE'S A MONSTER BEHIND YOU!

Knock, knock ...

Who's there?

Misty ...

Misty who?

Misty doorbell again!

Knock knock!

Who's there?

Wire.

Wire who?

Wire you asking me?

Knock, Knock ...

Who's there?

Voodoo.

Voodoo who?

Voodoo you think you are, asking all these questions?

Knock, knock ...

Who's there?

Igloo.

Igloo who?

Igloo knew Suzie like I know Suzie!

Knock, Knock ...

Who's there?

Says.

Says who?

Says me, that's who!

Knock, knock ...

Who's there?

Sorry.

Sorry who?

Sorry, wrong door!

KNOCK, KNOCK ...

Who's there?

YAH.

Yah who?

YAHOO! RIDE'em, COWBOY!

Knock, knock ...

Who's there?

Diesel.

Diesel who?

Diesel make you feel better!

KNOCK, KNOCK ...

Who's there?

ANITA.

Anita who?

ANITA YOU LIKE I NEED A HOLE IN THE HEAD!

Knock, knock ...

Who's there?

Aries.

Aries who?

Aries a reason I'm knocking at your door!

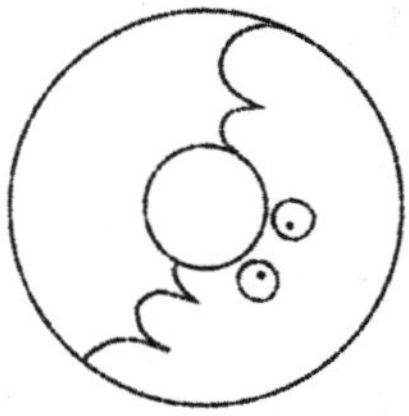

Knock, knock ...

Who's there?

Island.

Island who?

Island on your roof with my parachute!

Knock, knock ...

Who's there?

Olivia.

Olivia who?

Olivia, so get out of my house!

Knock, knock ...

Who's there?

Congo.

Congo who?

Congo into the woods, it's dangerous!

KNOCK, KNOCK ...

Who's there?

GLADYS ...

Gladys who?

GLADYS MY LAST JOKE!